POSH CLARET

The Remote Football Fan

"Posh Claret" first published in the United Kingdom in 2024 by Mike Stokes, 13 Beccelm Drive, Crowland, Lincolnshire, PE6 0AG

E-Mail mike.stokes@exportential.co.uk

© Mike Stokes 2024

Cover Photography by Nicola Auckland Photography, Kempton House, Kempton Way, Grantham, Lincolnshire, NG31 7LE

E-Mail nicola@nicolaaucklandphotography.co.uk

ISBN 978-1-7393342-2-2

INTRODUCTION

Although I have supported Burnley Football Club for well over 60 years, I have never lived within 100 miles of the place. Away games are often easy to reach, but home games have always entailed long and sometimes arduous journeys before and after the match.

Living so far away from "my club" has often resulted in a lack of news and information, at least in the pre-Internet days, and I usually found myself in a minority of one when my friends or work colleagues started to discuss football. When I lived in North Wales, the talk was all Liverpool, Everton and Manchester United. Then, after moving to Peterborough, I came across more fans of London clubs.

Because I have been so "unusual" in supporting a minority club, it has made me more memorable. Everyone knows me as "that Burnley supporter" and it is very often the first thing people mention when bumping into me – "I see Burnley did well at the weekend" or "whatever happened to Burnley last night?" I suppose that I tend to jog their memories by usually wearing a claret and blue scarf – even at formal business meetings.

The majority of Burnley fans live locally, many of them walk the short distance to Turf Moor and on match days they have finished their tea in time to go out for the night. I wanted to share my experiences as a fan who is every bit as loyal and passionate as the locals, even though each home game necessitates my driving 340 miles.

Supporting the Clarets has been a roller coaster of a ride, with some dismal days as well as a number of wonderful highlights. But this is not intended to be a history of Burnley FC, neither is it only about Burnley FC.

I inherited lots of things from my father – fidgeting too often, eating too quickly and farting too much all come to mind. But I am particularly grateful to him for passing on his passion for football and cricket. My dad was a life-long supporter of Arsenal but he encouraged me even after he discovered that I had broken with family tradition by <u>not</u> supporting Arsenal. Dad and I supported our respective teams with great vigour, but we both had a genuine interest in <u>all</u> football, not just in our own teams.

As well as describing my experiences whilst following Burnley, I have also included my memories of watching various non-league, league and international teams. This is intended to be a book not just for Burnley fans but also for any retro football supporters.

The quotations I have used are freely in circulation via the Internet. My apologies if I have been misled and accredited them to the wrong people!

I have not used photographs of recent shirts on the back cover because I refuse to support betting companies.

This does not pretend to be an informed critique of players past and present. It is instead an explanation of why an OAP continues to don a claret and blue scarf and drive 340 miles every other Saturday!

CONTENTS

1. WHY BURNLEY?
2. KEEPING IT LOCAL
3. SWINGING SIXTIES
4. TEAM OF THE SEVENTIES (Part 1)
5. KID IN A SWEET SHOP
6. TEAM OF THE SEVENTIES (Part 2)
7. PETERBOROUGH UNITED
8. AWFUL EIGHTIES
9. ORIENT GAME
10. WEMBLEY (SHERPA VAN)
11. WEMBLEY (PROMOTION 1)
12. DUBLIN CLARETS
13. ALLEN RYCROFT
14. RE-SCHEDULING
15. RECOVERY UNDER STAN
16. WHY POSH CLARET?
17. OVERSEAS GAMES
18. WEMBLEY (PROMOTION 2)
19. SEASON TICKETS IN THE PREMIER LEAGUE
20. LINCOLN CITY
21. ANTI-FOOTBALL
22. KOMPANY
23. WHY I DON'T HATE BASTARD ROVERS
24. NEVER MEET YOUR HEROES?
    APPENDIX

CHAPTER 1

WHY BURNLEY?

"A football team is like a piano. You need eight men to carry it and three who can play the damn thing". (Bill Shankly)

Without doubt, one of the secrets of our successful season was the harmonium in the dressing room." (Ivor Powell)

When I was a small boy, my dad (Jim Stokes) tried very hard to get me interested in football but, as I approached my seventh birthday in the autumn of 1959, it still hadn't clicked. But all that was to change within a few short weeks!

Dad had often got a ball out for us to play in our yard (which was quite large, with a convenient gate for a goal). But I never seemed particularly bothered, despite my dad's continuing encouragement.

Although we had no car, no fridge, no record player and no indoor loo, my parents were early to invest in a television. Back in the 1950s and early 1960s, there was very little televised football – maybe the odd England match, some European ties and, of course, the FA Cup Final. I remember we had a houseful of friends and relatives to watch the Final every year – my mother serving countless cups of tea – but I was never among the spectators.

It was difficult to keep in touch with scores and tables in those days. We had the morning papers, "Sports Report" on the radio and "Grandstand" on BBC television. At about 4.40pm every Saturday, "Grandstand" ran their teleprinter service, followed by the classified scores and tables. This is where my dad played his master-stroke, which led me to a life-long interest in football.

In order to get me interested, I was asked to watch the teleprinter sequence and then report back to him on how Arsenal had performed. I am not sure exactly when this started, but I recall reporting one week that Arsenal had beaten Blackpool, 2-1. I can confirm that would have been on 26th September 1959.

In October 1959, we moved home from St. Martins to Gobowen, still in Shropshire. There were two lads in our avenue – a couple of years older than me but both keen to welcome me into their "gang". Neville Edwards and Geoffrey Hughes were both keen on football and pretty much all of our time was spent playing football in the avenue, pausing only while the odd car came along. I think my willingness to play football was an important factor in my being accepted by these new friends.

Neville and Geoffrey were both Wolves fans and it was dawning on me that every boy needed to have his own team. My weekly exposure to the teleprinter slowly but surely exposed me to the range of clubs which were available to support. Then three things happened which determined which "my team" was going to be.

On 21st November 1959, I couldn't help but notice on the teleprinter that some team called Burnley had beaten Nottingham Forest by 8-0. My dad told me that was particularly impressive as Forest had won the FA Cup only a few months earlier. Incidentally, Jimmy Robson (who I would meet many years later) scored 5 goals for Burnley that day.

A couple of weeks later, on 12th December 1959, my dad's beloved Arsenal were thrashed 4-2 at home. And the victorious side was that team called Burnley again. On that occasion, John Connelly got a hat-trick.

A fortnight later, I received a football diary as one of my Christmas presents. The diary included drawings of footballers, in the various team colours. I particularly liked one of the teams' strip – claret shirts with blue sleeves and white shorts. And, would you believe it, the eye-catching strip belonged to that Burnley team again.

That was it – Burnley were going to be the team I followed, irrespective of where the team was located or how high they were in the league. When I discovered where the town of Burnley was situated, it did not put me off because, after all, my dad's team was even further away from us.

The first time I saw Burnley's name in a league table was after the 5-2 victory at West Ham on 2nd January 1960. They were in second place in the First Division, just behind Tottenham.

The plan to recruit me to the Arsenal cause had backfired but my dad was obviously pleased that I had picked my own team to follow, and that would lead to a general interest in the game that he enjoyed so much.

My love affair with the Clarets had begun and I was pleased that I had my own team to champion when talking football with Neville and Geoffrey.

Lots of people pick a team to support, either because of where they live, or because their dad supported the same team. I did neither!

CHAPTER 2

KEEPING IT LOCAL

"I spent a lot of money on booze, birds and fast cars. The rest I squandered." (George Best)

"Everything in our favour was against us." (Danny Blanchflower)

My dad did not pass his driving test until 1967 and he usually worked on Saturday mornings. So the chances of getting to any top-class football matches were slim. Really up until the late 1960s we had to make do with watching local football, which I continued to a certain extent for some years after.

By "local" I mean the Oswestry (Shropshire) area until the end of 1964, the Llandudno (North Wales) area from the start of 1965 until late 1972, Bromsgrove (Worcestershire) in 1973, and then the Peterborough area from 1973 to date.

I am afraid that some of these teams will not mean much to younger readers – indeed, some of them no longer exist – but they were an important part of my football education and enjoyment.

St.Martins

When I lived in the North Shropshire village of St.Martins, it was still very much concentrated on coal mining. My father and grandfather were employed by the National Coal Board, as were most of the men in the village. The tough miners from the village were difficult football opponents and were regular winners of the Whitchurch & District League and the Ethelston Cup.

My Dad had been a lively right half (midfielder for younger readers) for St.Martins and he had an impressive collection of medals and trophies – but he had stopped playing some time before my interest in the game.

I remember Terry Ellis on the right wing and brothers Derek and Travis Stokes (they must have been related to me but I have no idea how).

Most of the village seemed to attend the team's home fixtures on Saturday afternoons and I recall many carloads of us going to Whitchurch one early evening for the Ethelston Cup Final.

One game stands out for me, when St.Martins played a league match against Whixall. On the morning of the match, the regular centre forward cried off with an illness and, at such short notice, the only remedy was to bring Harold Jones out of retirement. Harold was portly (that's being polite) and hardly in the best of condition – but he was keen! St.Martins won the game 4-0 and Harold scored all four.

Gobowen

After we moved three miles from St.Martins to Gobowen, I was invited by Neville and Geoffrey to watch some of Gobowen's matches, also in the Whitchurch & District League.

Eric Stokes, my uncle, had moved from playing for St.Martins to representing Gobowen at left back and he played in one game I remember against Wem Town. I recall that Wem won the game 3-1 and that one of their goals was a quite spectacular long-distance own goal! I remember Vic Roberts was at right back and John Brown (our neighbour's son) at inside right.

Oswestry Town

There had been a football club in Oswestry since 1860, which made them one of the oldest clubs in the world. They had played in the Birmingham League until 1959, when they moved over to the Cheshire County League – and most of the games I saw at Victoria Road were in the Cheshire County League.

However, the first "proper" game I ever attended (where there were grandstands, corner flags, covered terraces and uniformed linesmen) was on 31st October 1959 between Oswestry Town and Evesham United in the FA Cup 4th Qualifying Round. I was taken along by my cousin, Norman Jones, and I remember the smell of embrocation (or "wintergreen" as it was known) as well as the fact that almost every man in the crowd was smoking. Evesham, in their red and white stripes, were no match for the blues of Oswestry, who ran out 4-1 winners.

The second match I attended was also an FA Cup match, in the 1st Qualifying Round on 10th September 1960 against Bromsgrove Rovers, again with cousin Norman. Bromsgrove were the first team I had seen in green shirts and an entertaining game ended 3-2 to Oswestry.

I saw a dramatic cup semi-final in April 1964 between Oswestry and Altrincham. Twice in the final five minutes an Altrincham defender lumped the ball high towards the Oswestry goal and twice the home keeper was dazzled by the low sun and punched the ball into his own net!

I can't remember many of the Oswestry players – only the goalkeeper, Charlie Hughes, full back Gerry Broadhead (against whom my dad had played), a sharp and direct forward called Tony Broadhead (no relation to Gerry), a striker called Mel Ryan and an inside forward called Brian Edgeley.

After moving to North Wales, I only saw Oswestry Town play once more – against Nantwich Town in April 1972. They had financial problems and had to leave their Victoria Road ground. Eventually they merged with TNS, a very successful club, who seem to win the Welsh Premier League every year.

Wrexham

The nearest Football League club to our home in North Shropshire was Wrexham, about 13 miles away. It was still our nearest ground after we moved to Llandudno Junction, although that journey was over 50 miles.

I was born at Chirk, which is less than 10 miles from Wrexham – and I was in good company. An early Welsh football legend, Billy Meredith, had been born in the house later occupied by my dad's aunty.

My first visit to the Racecourse was on 9th January 1963 for a 3rd Round FA Cup tie between Third Division Wrexham and Liverpool of the First Division. This was my first experience of floodlit football and I thoroughly enjoyed it. I went with my dad and two of my uncles, one of whom decided that we should leave before the end, to beat the worst of the traffic. We left with Liverpool leading 2-0 and when we arrived at home my mother said "that sounded entertaining with three goals". Our early departure resulted in our missing Liverpool's third goal – and I have not left a game early since then.

Wrexham was obviously the place to be for goals that season – my second visit in April 1963 saw Crystal Palace beating Ken Barnes' home side 4-3.

After leaving West Ham, John Bond played for Torquay United and I saw him playing at Wrexham in March 1966, in a Division 4 fixture. Bond played a tidy game, nothing like as flamboyant as he was when he became a manager.

I attended quite a few matches at Wrexham, right up until I left North Wales in late 1972. These matches included normal league and cup games involving Wrexham, plus a number of representative games.

I saw the Wales v Northern Ireland game in February 1968 and I was pleased to see three Burnley players (Willie Irvine, Alex Elder and Sammy Todd) in the visitors' side.

A Welsh Cup match against Cardiff City gave me an early view of a young John Toshack, who was clearly destined for greater things.

We were treated to the cream of English football in October 1968 when Wales Under 23s played England Under 23s, the visitors winning 3-1.

Some of these games involved travelling in my dad's car, but quite a few were trips organised by my school and, later, by work colleagues. Buses from work enabled me to attend Wrexham's European Cup Winners Cup ties against FC Zurich and Hajduk Split. In those days, Wrexham's ground featured a strange-looking stand which was almost suspended behind the goal. The story was that the club had bought it from a local cinema. Goodness knows what today's health and safety experts would have made of it, as it looked decidedly precarious to me!

The last time I attended a game at The Racecourse was the occasion of Stan Ternent's turnaround in March 1999 – more of which later.

Shrewsbury Town

Although Wrexham was the nearest league club to our home in North Shropshire, it was actually quicker to get to Gay Meadow, the home of Shrewsbury Town. There was a very regular rail service between Gobowen and Shrewsbury, so my mate Geoffrey and I used to go occasionally to watch them playing in the Third Division. Neville didn't join us because he was always playing in goal for the school team (he was one of the ball boys at the 1966 World Cup Final and I recognised him on tv, returning the ball with his left-handed bowling action).

I was something of a good luck charm for Shrewsbury, as I never saw them lose. My highlights were 6-1 victories over Workington and Wrexham. At the time Shrewsbury employed a player-manager, the record-breaking goalscorer, Arthur Rowley. Arthur was often listed on the match programme but I never saw him play.

Only once did I see the ball booted over the covered terrace and into the river behind. I understand that on matchdays the club engaged a boatman who retrieved any lost balls in his coracle. Regular spectators were the students at the adjacent art college – they would hang out of the windows to try and catch the action below.

Borough United

In January 1965, we moved from North Shropshire to Llandudno Junction in North Wales. My dad had been promoted to Depot Manager in the NCB and he managed coal depots in Llandudno and Colwyn Bay. Llandudno Junction was situated between those two towns and it was also only a mile or so from Conwy. It also housed one of the best non-league football clubs in Wales.

In 1952, two local sides (Conwy Borough and Llandudno Junction) decided to merge and they called the new club Borough United. The new club acquitted itself very well, culminating in the winning of the Welsh Cup in 1963. They beat league club Newport County in the two-legged final and so qualified to play in the European Cup Winners Cup in the 1963-64 season. They beat Sliema Wanderers and then were knocked out by Slovan Bratislava.

Borough United's ground was only ten minutes' walk from our new home and my dad was able to join me there even after working in the morning. As a result, we hardly missed a home game between January 1965 and May 1966.

My first Borough game was a Welsh Cup tie in which Llangollen were beaten 8-2 and this was followed by a league game where Prestatyn were thrashed 7-2. In this latter game, Gerry Duffy scored the only double hat-trick (6 goals) that I have ever seen. Cup ties against league teams were special occasions, although I recall a 5-2 defeat against Chester in the Welsh Cup. Amongst Borough's players were the brothers Keith and Mike Pritchard and I later played cricket alongside them both. One of my school teachers, Dyfed Elias, became Borough's captain but my dad and I both liked the left winger, Reg Hunter. Reg had been a "Busby Babe" and had a spell with Wrexham before joining Borough. He was also a mean left arm swing bowler – but I don't remember him ever taking my wicket!

I managed to catch a few away games, usually semi-finals or finals, one being a North Wales Challenge Cup semi-final against Portmadoc, at Caernarvon. Portmadoc were led by former Welsh international Mel Charles and they led 2-1 with only a couple of minutes to go. Keith Pritchard then broke away twice to win the tie for Borough. I met Mel Charles some years later at a sportsman's lunch and I reminded him about this game. He was very friendly and didn't seem to mind that I had brought up a Portmadoc defeat!

I hardly saw any Borough matches after the end of the 1965-66 season because I played on Saturday afternoons myself. And then, at the end of the 1966-67 season the owners of their ground evicted the club and they quickly disappeared.

Bangor City

Another local non-league club had won the Welsh Cup in 1962 and represented Wales in the European Cup Winners Cup in the 1962-63 season. Bangor City received a tough draw, against the Italians AC Napoli, although Bangor were eliminated only after a third match.

My dad got his first car in 1967 so we were no longer dependent on lifts or public transport to get to matches. As well as attending league matches more often, we also picked up on the fact that Bangor City had joined the new Northern Premier League.

Mick McGrath (a former Blackburn Rovers player) was the manager when I used to watch Bangor, but the highlight was the free-scoring strike partnership of Jim Conde and George Morton. There was plenty of entertainment in those days at Farrar Road – I remember in April 1969 a 3-3 draw with Wigan Athletic being followed 2 days later by a 2-3 defeat to Scarborough.

Not long afterwards I attended a special match at Farrar Road between Wales and Manchester United, to celebrate the Investiture of Prince Charles as the Prince of Wales. The train between Llandudno Junction and Bangor was heaving with fans, the game was lacklustre and United won 2-0.

At Bangor, I watched the Wales Schools v England Schools match in 1970, mainly because one of my best friends, Rob Gawne, was in goal for Wales. Unfortunately, Wales lost the game, 5-3.

My last visits to see Bangor were during the autumn of 1972, not long before I moved to Bromsgrove.

Bromsgrove Rovers

Whilst I was studying for an accountancy qualification, I took the opportunity to watch all the league teams close to Bromsgrove – and my experiences of those games are covered later in this book. I also managed to watch a few games involving the local non-league club, Bromsgrove Rovers. I particularly remember three games at Bromsgrove, none of which they lost.
The first was a dour defensive struggle against local rivals, Kidderminster Harriers, as both sides sought Southern League silverware.
The second game was a Border Counties Floodlit League encounter against one of my previous favourites, Oswestry Town. Poor Oswestry put up a dismal show and were well beaten 7-3.
My biggest thrill came in my third match at Bromsgrove, because I got to see Merthyr Tydfil's player-manager, the legendary John Charles. John must have been 41 or 42 at the time but he was still a master at receiving a ball, instantly controlling it and then laying it off to a colleague. Despite John's best efforts, his team were beaten in the last minute, 5-4.

Stamford Town

Whilst both of my daughters grew up as Peterborough fans, they both used to come along with me and support our local non-league clubs.
Stamford was a homely club and often made good progress in the FA Vase, actually winning it one year.

They also had a good track record in attracting high-quality opposition for pre-season friendlies, like Brian Clough's Nottingham Forest. Unfortunately one of these friendlies had a very sad outcome.

Alan Davies had played really well on the wing for Manchester United in the 1983 FA Cup Final and shortly afterwards made his debut for Wales. He came to Stamford for a pre-season friendly match and broke his leg, never to be the same player again. Davies took his own life at the age of only 30.

Spalding United

My days watching Spalding coincided with the appearance of free-scoring Carl Shutt, who moved to Sheffield Wednesday and Leeds United in later years. At a mid-week friendly between Spalding and Peterborough, I sat behind the Posh manager, John Wile. Wile's only bellowed instruction to his team consisted of "put it up on Hank's chest". Wile had signed the ex-Burnley striker, Ray Hankin, the week before. Spalding won, 1-0.

The grandstand at Spalding had wooden floorboards and the fans would stamp their feet to generate a bit of noise. My elder daughter would have been 5 or 6 at the time and she thought it was wonderful to be able to stamp her feet without being scolded!

Holbeach United

Another local team we supported in the early 1980s was Holbeach United. We enjoyed going there because we could almost get all the way around the ground without any barriers or restrictions. We would time our

tour of the ground so that we ended up by the cozy clubhouse just in time for a halftime brew.
The Tigers were a very homely club and my highlight of watching them was an FA Cup 1st Round tie against Wrexham, played at Peterborough.

Although the majority of this book covers my experiences whilst watching Football League and Premier League clubs, I have some very fond memories of watching non-league football. As well as the clubs mentioned above, I also saw single matches at **Chirk AAA** (North Wales), **Colwyn Bay** (North Wales), **Llandudno** (North Wales), **Crowland Town** (Peterborough), **Eye United** (Peterborough) and **Yaxley** (Peterborough). I strongly recommend to any fans of top-flight clubs that you occasionally take in a match at your local club. And there is no VAR to worry about, either!

My own performances in local North Wales football were very unspectacular. I was a centre half, who was ok in the air but too slow on the deck. More importantly for the 1960s and early 1970s, I wasn't hard (or dirty) enough to make progress.

I only played against two international players – Joey Jones, who was no better than the rest of us at the same age, and Mickey Thomas, who was much better than the rest of us. It was no surprise to see how Mickey progressed,

CHAPTER 3

SWINGING SIXTIES

"My heart has only one colour – blue and white." (Joao Pinto)

"He covers every blade of grass out there …. but that is only because his first touch is so crap." (Dave Jones)

The 1960s were dubbed the "Swinging Sixties" because of the exciting introduction of vibrant pop music, exotic fashions and fascinating characters. It was a wonderful time to be alive and I can tell you that when it came to "Sex and Drugs and Rock 'n' Roll" …. I read about them all!

The 1960s were also wonderful times for Burnley fans, as the club enjoyed lofty league positions, exhilarating cup runs and even European campaigns. And I chose to follow the club just as this run of success began.

Champions

My first part-season as a Clarets fan could not have been better. At the turn of the year, we were second in the table, competing with Tottenham and Wolves. Wolves were seeking a third consecutive title and were in with a good chance of a league and cup double. Very occasionally, the goals from Burnley's games would appear at the end of news bulletins or on "Sportsview", a midweek programme on the BBC. Otherwise, my only sources of news were "Grandstand" on a Saturday or the morning newspapers. Burnley, Spurs and Wolves vied neck-and-neck with each other and, despite a 6-1 hammering at Wolves in late March, we were in the frame as the season reached its climax.

A set-back occurred when we sacrificed a 3-0 lead to draw with Blackburn in the FA Cup, losing the replay at Ewood Park. But at least we could then concentrate on the league. Spurs and Wolves completed their fixtures on 30th April, but Burnley had one game left, at Manchester City on the Monday evening. Anything other than a Burnley win would result in the title going to Wolves, but a Burnley victory would bring the title to Turf Moor – despite the fact that Burnley had not topped the table at any stage prior to the last game.

I was only 7 years old and I wasn't allowed to stay up to find out the result, so it was the following morning when I found out that a 2-1 victory had resulted in Burnley being crowned Champions of England. Although I was young and had only been a fan for a few months it was really exciting to go to school and greet my Wolves-supporting friends.

Football League Division 1 : 1959-60			P	W	D	L	Pts
1.	Burnley		42	24	7	11	55
2.	Wolverhampton W.		42	24	6	12	54
3.	Tottenham Hotspur		42	21	11	10	53
4.	West Bromwich Albion		42	19	11	12	49

Europe

As the reigning champions of England, Burnley participated in the European Cup during the 1960-61 season. There was hardly any televised football in those days so I looked forward to a special treat in November 1960, when the BBC were showing the Burnley v Reims game live. Unfortunately, my mother insisted on watching ITV first, so I missed the first 30 minutes but I was pleased with the 2-0 result. We beat the French team on aggregate but came a cropper in the Quarter Final, losing to Hamburg over 2 legs. I seem to recall that the second leg match in Hamburg was shown on tv, with an early kick-off for a midweek game. A disappointing outcome, but a tie which would lead to my making a presentation to a Burnley player over 40 years later!

That season was dominated by the Tottenham double-winning side, although Burnley's fourth position in the league, alongside 2 domestic semi-finals, was a fine effort. A year after being champions, Burnley were still very much among the leading pack.

During the summer of 1961, I got to meet a Burnley player for the first time – and I got to play against him. Billy Marshall was visiting relatives very close to where my grandparents lived. While he was there, he went out for a kickabout on the local recreation ground known as the bullring. Within minutes, every lad had joined the group and we were all put into teams (Billy picked one team and my uncle Eric picked the other). As an 8 year old, I was one of the last players to be picked, and Billy failed to pick me for his side. At least I got his autograph though.

FA Cup Final

The season after Spurs' double, Burnley very nearly repeated the achievement. We hit the top of the league in early September and pretty much stayed there all season, until Ipswich's strong finish pipped us at the post. My dad and I had been to visit my grandfather in Wrexham hospital on the final Saturday of the league season and a neighbour offered us a lift home. As we got in the car, the driver informed us that Ipswich had just won the First Division, as Burnley had only drawn with Chelsea.

Perhaps the bigger disappointment for me at that time was our failure to lift the FA Cup. We had an excellent run to the final and I then had the pleasure of watching all the pre-match build up, as "my team" participated in one of the best finals for years. But we lost to Spurs, and I cried.

Football League Division 1 : 1961-62						
		P	W	D	L	Pts
1.	Ipswich Town	42	24	8	10	56
2.	Burnley	42	21	11	10	53
3.	Tottenham Hotspur	42	21	10	11	52
4.	Everton	42	20	11	11	51

Anfield 1962

November 3rd, 1962 was an unforgettable day for me – the first time I saw Burnley playing in the flesh. It was an early tenth birthday present, which my dad organised with a Liverpool-supporting friend, Jimmy Brimmage. My mother and sister came on the train and ferry with us, as they planned to take advantage of the shopping facilities. Burnley had made a decent start to the season, sitting in the top 3, while Liverpool had found it tough to settle after their promotion the previous season. I remember the long queues outside the ground (43,000 attended) and the excitement as we got near to the turnstiles. Once inside the ground, the noise level increased as 3pm approached, and then white-shirted Jimmy Adamson led the visitors onto the pitch, to be greeted by boos from the home fans.
The match was accompanied by the Liverpool fans' new chant – "Liverpool" clap, clap, clap – "Liverpool" clap, clap, clap. The early exchanges were pretty even but then Burnley took the lead with a well-struck shot from the edge of the penalty area by Ray Pointer. My first-ever Burnley goal had been scored by the player I still regard as the finest number nine who ever drew breath!
Early in the second half, the home side equalised through Ian St.John but Burnley secured the points with a fine headed goal by Andy Lochhead. One of my chief takeaways from the match came from our full back, Alex

Elder. Until then, I had regarded full backs almost as second class players but Elder demonstrated great skill and changed my thinking entirely.

So, I had seen my team playing for the first time. Going back on the train to Shropshire, I just knew that Burnley would always be near the top of the table and, of course, we would always beat Liverpool. Ah well ….

Burnley finished third that season, behind Everton and our old foes, Tottenham. Newly-promoted Liverpool finished a very creditable eighth and they had the satisfaction of beating Burnley in an FA Cup replay.

Football League Division 1 : 1962-63						
		P	W	D	L	Pts
1.	Everton	42	25	11	6	61
2.	Tottenham Hotspur	42	23	9	10	55
3.	Burnley	42	22	10	10	54
4.	Leicester City	42	20	12	10	52

Molineux

At the start of the 1963-64 season, it was decided that my dad and I would make the occasional trip to Wolverhampton with my uncle Eric and his work colleague, Ted Williams (who was the driver). It was agreed that we would pick matches which involved our own teams, plus the occasional fixture of interest. The journey from North Shropshire was over 50 miles, probably taking 2 hours in those days before motorways and ring roads.

The first match we attended was in late August 1963, Stoke City being the visitors. Stoke were newly-promoted and featured in their ranks the legendary Stanley

Matthews. I was looking forward, not just to seeing a top-tier match, but also to getting a glimpse of the old maestro, who must have been 48 years old by then. Just before the teams took to the field, the team news was announced, and at number 7 for Stoke was Keith Bebbington, not Matthews. Now Keith Bebbington was a decent winger, but he wasn't the genius I hoped we would see. Wolves won 2-1 and I never did get to see "The Wizard Of The Dribble".

In November of that year, our second trip to Molineux saw the FA Cup holders, Manchester United, well beaten (2-0) by an impressive Wolves side. It was my first view of Denis Law and Bobby Charlton, both of whom were impressive but without scoring.

The following month, we got to see my dad's team, Arsenal, get a hard-earned 2-2 draw at Molineux. My first impression as Arsenal ran out was Ian Ure's shock of blond hair. So, by Christmas we had seen three First Division games and I had really enjoyed myself getting to see players who had only appeared in newspapers and magazines up to this point. But when the tickets for our next Molineux match arrived, I got really excited – Wolves v Burnley in March 1964.

Burnley got a well-deserved 1-1 draw from this game, but my big memory was my first view of Willie Morgan, one of the most skilful players to don a claret and blue shirt. There were not many Clarets fans present but I managed to make a fair old racket with my new wooden rattle.

One of the Wolves players who impressed me most was a young striker named Ted Farmer. Unfortunately, his career was ended early by injury.

We only went to one Wolves game in the 1964-65 season, fairly early on against Blackpool, who featured the immaculate Jimmy Armfield and a lively youngster, Alan Ball. Both players would be included in England's World Cup squad in 1966.

My only other game during this mid-Sixties period was at Coventry, their first match in the Second Division after gaining promotion, in August 1964. I was very impressed by all the innovative things Jimmy Hill had introduced at Highfield Road, especially "Radio Sky Blue" which made all other tannoy announcements sound like the shipping forecast! Coventry beat Plymouth 2-0 but it could have been more.

Mid Table

After four incredibly successful league seasons, Burnley re-grouped, finishing 9th and 12th respectively in 1963-64 and 1964-65, as Liverpool, Manchester United and Leeds United progressed. The older players from earlier in the decade (Adamson, McIlroy, Cummings) players with injuries like Pointer and sold players like Connelly, were being replaced by younger players such as Morgan, Irvine, Lochhead, O'Neil and Coates.

My dad was promoted to a new position with the NCB, which meant that he moved to North Wales, and we followed him in January 1965. We still had no car and, after moving to a brand new bungalow, let's just say that finances were tough for a while. Following the game at Wolves in 1964, I didn't get to see Burnley again for over four years. I just had to rely upon newspaper reports and the occasional mention on the television and radio.

Back Up To Third

Burnley's forward line for most of the 1965-66 season was Morgan, Lochhead, Irvine, Harris and Coates. With Brian O'Neil driving forward from midfield, this was a very potent attack and this was the main reason why Burnley finished a very creditable third, level on points with runners up, Leeds.

I'm afraid that "Match Of The Day" didn't move to BBC1 until the start of the 1966-67 season, so I had very few glimpses of this excellent side – maybe the odd 30 seconds at the end of a news bulletin. I would have loved to have seen some of Willie Irvine's 29 goals that year.

	Football League Division 1 : 1965-66					
		P	W	D	L	Pts
1.	Liverpool	42	26	9	7	61
2.	Leeds United	42	23	9	10	55
3.	Burnley	42	24	7	11	55
4.	Manchester United	42	18	15	9	51

They Think It's All Over

I can't just scroll through the Sixties without mentioning the 1966 World Cup. It was closely followed, even by fans in North Wales, and the World Cup fever certainly caught up with us all. I didn't see any of the games in the flesh, but I was an avid TV watcher, hardly missing a minute of the action.

I must nail my colours firmly to the mast and declare that

- I was born in Wales
- had I been good enough to play international football it would have been for Wales
- I support Wales against England whenever they meet (in any sport, not just football)
- but I support England against everyone else

Having the World Cup finals in England was very exciting. I was 13 and "football daft" so I couldn't get enough of the build-up. I had a booklet with a fixture guide free in a magazine.

Unlike recent World Cups, in 1966 there were often several games played at the same time. As we were watching England play Argentina in the quarter final, we were only aware of Portugal's 5-3 victory over North Korea from the occasional score flash as the goals rained in.

The atmosphere in the country as the tournament progressed was electric and the final was unforgettable. We had about ten watching the game on our television and a memory I have is of our next door neighbour going outside on his lawn during extra time as he could no longer handle the tension.

To win a World Cup, you normally need 3 or 4 absolutely world class players and then some pretty good players alongside them. At the time, Banks, Wilson, Moore and Charlton were the best players in the world in their positions and I don't believe England have been able to say that since. A fully-fit Jimmy Greaves might have made that five world-class players. I thoroughly enjoyed seeing Eusebio, Florian Albert, Franz Beckenbauer and the

Russian, Eduard Malofeev. My only regret from that tournament is that we didn't get to see a fit Pelé, as he was mercilessly clogged out of the finals.

England number one in the world, Burnley number three in England. Can't be bad!

Up until England's World Cup win, I had occasionally bought a copy of Charles Buchan's Football Monthly, an excellent magazine covering all aspects of football. From July 1966, my dad placed a regular order so I took the magazine every month. It was about that time that I noticed an advert for football scarves from a place at Driffield, Yorkshire. You just could not buy a claret and blue scarf in North Wales and, at that time, I had still not been to Burnley. So I persuaded my parents to pay for the postal order and off it went to Driffield. When the scarf arrived, it was somewhat smaller than I had expected – but I finally had something in my team's colours.

Europe Again

Burnley's third place finish meant that we took part in the 1966-67 Inter-Cities Fairs Cup tournament. This was a very successful campaign, beating Stuttgart, Lausanne and Napoli before losing to Eintracht Frankfurt. Maybe our European exertions took their toll, as Burnley had to settle for 14th place in the league.

The saddest event took place when Willie Irvine had his leg broken in an FA Cup replay at Everton. He had been a prolific scorer but he was never the same player after the breakage.

After this season, Burnley would not play competitive European football again for over 50 years.

Repeatedly 14th

In terms of Burnley's success, the four seasons between 1966 and 1970 were very similar. In all four seasons we weren't good enough to challenge for European spots, but neither were we in relegation trouble. So, we finished 14th in all four seasons.

But in terms of my own involvement, things were starting to look up. In April 1967 my dad passed his driving test – but his first car was a nightmare and he was never confident enough to take my mum on shopping expeditions to Liverpool or to take me to league football matches. Dad solved the problem by buying a brand new Hillman Minx in early 1968.

Our first football journey in the new car was to Everton in early May 1968, against Stoke City. Everton were building a more than useful side at that time, and ran out comfortable winners, by 3-0. That was our first experience of a youngster offering to "look after your car" until the end of the game. Thankfully my dad had been tipped off by his friend in the local constabulary, so he gave the lad half of the money up front and the other half when we got back.

During the summer of 1968, we went to Blackpool for two long weekends (enjoying Tommy Cooper and Ken Dodd, among others) so my dad was building up his driving experience. While we were in Blackpool, I saw a small stand near the seafront which was selling novelties, "kiss me quick" hats and other items. Among these were badges in football clubs' colours with the club name emblazoned across the centre. I was delighted to find a Burnley badge among them – this would never have been the case back in North Wales.

Our next match was an evening August fixture at Goodison Park between an improving Everton and a Burnley side which was flattered by the 0-3 scoreline. We looked like conceding every time Everton attacked – with Alan Ball pulling all the strings. Even so, it was still a great thrill to see my Burnley heroes live – perhaps this is difficult for local fans to appreciate, as they see them regularly.

We tried Anfield next. We watched Liverpool beat Leicester 4-0, a game where the first £100,000 teenager, Alun Evans, made his debut. Those few trips to Merseyside, and a trip to Old Trafford in October 1968 (when the home fans just chanted "Champions Of Europe" all through the game) had whetted our appetites, so I decided to put in that all-important request – could we go to Turf Moor?

My parents decided that my first trip to Burnley should be my birthday present, so the day after my sixteenth birthday I got to pay homage to my footballing gods at our home ground for the first time. My dad shared the driving with Ken Hughes, a family friend, whose son completed our party of four. Our tickets included a tour of the ground – which clubs don't seem to do on matchdays any more.

In 1968 the old main stand was still standing (pre Bob Lord stand) and we were able to park right outside the ground at about 10.30am in time to meet our tour guide. We were shown the boardroom, the changing rooms and the physio room (which included meeting the legendary "bucket and sponge man", Jimmy Holland). Most exciting of all, was the walk from the changing rooms and onto the hallowed turf. After supporting the club for nearly 9 years, I had finally arrived at my equivalent of Mecca. We were given a few recent programmes and then went off for lunch before the big game.

As luck would have it, Burnley's opponents in my first Turf Moor game were my dad's team, Arsenal. Unfortunately, a Jimmy Robertson strike on the half hour was enough to win the game for the Gunners but I had seen a number of Burnley players for the first time (Wilf Wrigley, Eric Probert, Mick Docherty, Colin Blant and the club legend, Martin Dobson).

A couple of weeks after the Arsenal game, Burnley lost a League Cup semi-final tie against Swindon Town – who then went on to beat Arsenal in the final.

One of my mother's work colleagues helped to run a coach service from Llandudno to all of Manchester United's home matches. I managed to get myself on the coach for the United v Burnley League Cup evening match in October 1969 – just myself and 30-odd United fans! We lost by one goal to nil and we didn't disgrace ourselves, although I got some intense earache from the home fans every time we dared to foul their darlings! Unfortunately, my claret and blue bobble cap was snatched outside the ground by a friendly local, who quickly disappeared down a side street.

In November 1969, my dad and I saw Burnley visiting that season's champions, Everton. Ralph Coates scored a good goal but the Kendal-Ball-Harvey midfield won the game for the home side, 2-1.

On 3rd January 1970, I made my first visit to Burnley by train. A fellow Burnley fan from the Llandudno area, Les Williams, joined me on the long journey from Llandudno Junction, changing in Manchester. On the second train we were befriended by some fans bedecked in the colours of our opponents, Wolves. They were pleasant company, or at least they were before the game. We sat in the relatively new Cricket Field stand and we were well entertained as the Clarets won the FA Cup 3rd round tie, 3-0. The Wolves fans weren't quite so pleasant on the return journey, one lanky skinhead being particularly hostile.

As the fan of a so-called "small" club, I had to be careful and keep my eye on situations where I could be confronted by large groups of hostile fans, and not just fans of our opponents on that particular day. Railway stations could get a bit lively as various fans were changing trains and I was never afraid to display my claret and blue colours.

The victory over Wolves resulted in our being drawn away at Chelsea in the 4th round – a difficult tie as Chelsea were in the top three at the time. We came from behind with two Martin Dobson goals in the final ten minutes to earn a replay on the following Tuesday night. "Can we go?", I asked my dad, who surprisingly agreed.

At lunchtime, my dad made a surprise appearance at my school, to say that he had been called away on a work matter and that he therefore couldn't make the trip to Burnley. But he offered to pay the petrol if any of my friends fancied being a chauffeur for the evening. My mate, Rob Gawne (the one who played in goal for Wales Schools), offered to use his car so the two of us, plus Les

Williams, and Francis Graves ("Fritz"), set off straight after school.

The journey became more difficult as the fog got progressively worse and we ended up getting lost near Blackburn. We missed the first five minutes of the game as we squeezed with difficulty into the Longside. After 90 minutes, the game stood at 1-1 but then Chelsea scored two extra time goals to take the tie. They went on to lift the trophy after a replay against Leeds.

We left Burnley at 10pm and headed through ever-denser fog towards North Wales. When stopping at a motorway service station, we were threatened by some layabouts from Glasgow which hardly made the journey any easier. By the time we got home it was after 1am – and we were out of the FA Cup.

My final game of the 1969-70 season was a very entertaining 3-3 draw at the home of Manchester United. Steve Kindon and David Thomas (2) had given visiting Burnley a 3-1 halftime lead, demonstrating genuine pace. But, after the break, United's forwards (Best, Charlton, Law and our old friend Willie Morgan) wore us down and they clawed back the deficit.

So, for the fourth consecutive season, Burnley finished in 14th place, which was respectable if not spectacular. During the previous couple of seasons, a number of very promising young players had been introduced and the future of the club looked very positive. In fact, our team manager, Jimmy Adamson, forecasted that Burnley would be "The Team Of The Seventies".

CHAPTER 4

TEAM OF THE SEVENTIES (Part 1)

"Davie Hay still has a fresh pair of legs up his sleeve." (John Greig)

"I wouldn't say that I was the best manager in the business, but I was in the top one." (Brian Clough)

Having won the FA Youth Cup in 1968, and having bought some very tasty young players (Colin Waldron, Jim Thomson, Frank Casper, Martin Dobson, Geoff Nulty and Doug Collins), Burnley had every reason to look forward to the 1970s with great optimism. The decade was certainly eventful, but not always in the way that Jimmy Adamson had foreseen!

Disappointing Start

In September 1970, I left school and joined the appliances manufacturer, Hotpoint, initially as a trainee cost accountant. As we will see, I was to remain with them for over 30 years – but not as an accountant.

The 1970-71 season started in the worst possible manner, Burnley failing to win any of their first 14 games and finding themselves at the foot of the table. I saw the second game of the season, a very creditable 1-1 draw at Everton, who were the reigning champions. There was no indication then of how badly things would turn out.

The season was dismal, but I can't remember why I didn't get to any other games that year. I know my dad was particularly busy and often worked on Saturdays at that time and I didn't pass my driving test until April 1971. Just before my driving test, one of my cricket friends, Tommy Marshall, offered to drive me to see the Burnley v Blackpool game on April 10th. Accompanied by two other friends, we set off in good time. As we approached the Manchester area, Tommy's mini started to struggle so we checked in to a repair centre, where we learned that the car could not be patched up before 4pm. The four of us then went to see Manchester United lose at home to Derby County. We travelled by bus back to the repaired car, to learn that we had missed Burnley's fifth victory of the season.

That first campaign of the seventies was a huge disappointment and we were deservedly relegated along with Blackpool. It was my first experience of relegation and I didn't like it. I have never hidden the fact that I support Burnley, so everyone knows – schoolfriends, college mates, work colleagues etc. I had been mercilessly taunted and teased all season and it was difficult to retort, as I knew we were so poor. I had a regular pint pot at the Hotpoint Social Club, engraved with "Mike Burnley", and the night we were finally relegated my pot was draped in black cloth by someone. Folks can be cruel!

	Football League Division 1 : 1970-71					
		P	W	D	L	Pts
19.	Ipswich Town	42	12	10	20	34
20.	West Ham United	42	10	14	18	34
21.	Burnley	42	7	13	22	27
22.	Blackpool	42	4	15	23	23

It seemed so strange having to listen to the second section of results on a Saturday evening to get my team's score. And, although we didn't exactly light up Division Two in that first season, there was the feeling that our stay outside Division One would only be temporary.

Four times during the 1971-72 season I joined the Hotpoint bus to Old Trafford. I didn't have to drive, so that meant a few pints in "The Quadrant", just around the corner from Old Trafford Cricket Ground. And, although I was definitely not a United fan, I got to see some excellent games that season.

Strangely, United's first game that season was at Anfield, as they weren't allowed to use their own ground for a few games. It was against the previous season's double winners, Arsenal, and United ran out comfortable winners by 3-1.

I was then treated to a masterclass from George Best, as he took West Ham apart and scored a hat-trick against Bobby Moore and co. I also caught the Manchester United v Spurs fixture, which was always entertaining and in November 1971 United won 3-1.

My final trip to Old Trafford that season was to see the local derby, United v City. The visitors were in with a good shout for the Division One title in April 1972 and they prevailed, 3-1, with Colin Bell outstanding.

My only visit to Burnley in that first season after relegation was in November, when the Clarets played Swindon Town, managed by Dave Mackay and featuring the future Burnley star, Peter Noble. Burnley failed to impress and lost 2-1. We made a family trip out of that fixture, my dad joining me at Turf Moor whilst my mother went around the shops (she loved Burnley market).

It was an inconsistent season, one of the highlights being a victory over the eventual champions, Norwich City. We were never out of the top ten, yet we failed to threaten the top three or four. We did finish the season very strongly, though, and won our last six games – which augured very well for the following season.

Hello, Hello – Burnley Are Back, Burnley Are Back

I have very fond memories of the 1972-73 season. Somehow or another, I managed to attend 37 games, of which 14 involved Burnley.

I started off the season with my two final trips on the Hotpoint bus to Old Trafford, firstly to see United draw with Leicester City and then to attend the Bobby Charlton Testimonial match, United v Celtic.

A massive crowd had gone to Old Trafford to say thank you to Charlton and to no doubt see him score one of his specials into the top corner. Celtic played their part, backing off Charlton when he looked like getting in a shot. And his team-mates spent the whole evening gently rolling passes into his path. The trouble was that Bobby hit everything except the goal and at the end of the evening it finished 0-0.

My first trip to Turf Moor that season was in August for an attractive fixture with Aston Villa. We absolutely took them apart, scoring some very good goals and we won 4-1. I recall that the game was shown by ITV the following afternoon and a number of punters were backing us as possible promotion contenders.

We wobbled a bit in our next two home matches, drawing luckily against QPR and hanging on to win 4-3 against Blackpool, having been 4-0 up at one stage. The police were keen to avoid trouble at the railway station after the Blackpool game and one officer asked me where I was going. When I replied "Llandudno" he barked "don't get funny with me son!"

My parents took me to Bromsgrove on October 14th, to make arrangements for my accommodation in the town during my forthcoming stint at the local college. After our final meeting, we returned to the car to hear that Burnley had beaten Sheffield Wednesday and had gone to the top of the table. "Match Of The Day" covered the game later that evening, featuring a superb strike by Leighton James. We could start to believe!

A Paul Fletcher hat-trick made for a smooth victory over Cardiff – but then we came a cropper. We had started the season with 16 games unbeaten but unfancied Orient came to Turf Moor and won 2-1. It acted as a wake-up call and we didn't lose another league game in 1972.

On Boxing Day, Les Williams' dad offered to drive us to the away fixture at Blackpool – which happened to be his team. Blackpool had a decent side and we had to work hard for a 2-1 victory, with Frank Casper bagging both goals. A frustrating 2-2 draw with Fulham took us to the end of the year. I had been able to borrow my dad's car for that one – and, in fairness, he would often let me do so after then.

In November 1972 I moved to Bromsgrove to attend the local college and I have covered most of my football memories from my time there in the next chapter. But I was able to continue my support for the Clarets from 130 miles away.

The first game I saw in 1973 was only a short bus ride away for me – from Bromsgrove to Birmingham, where Burnley were visiting Aston Villa. When I moved to Bromsgrove, everyone assumed my claret and blue scarf (plus hat and shoulder bag) signified that I was a Villa fan. For a few weeks before we met Villa, their fans were telling me what they would do to us when Burnley visited Villa Park. We responded by putting in one of the finest away performances I have ever seen from Burnley.

I arrived at Villa Park and was approached by a man who said that he had a spare ticket for the stand, as his mate couldn't make it. I bought the ticket and found myself sitting next to the chap who sold me the ticket. Imagine his surprise when I leapt to my feet with a loud roar as the Burnley team emerged from the tunnel!

Villa were in third place at the time, but Burnley outclassed them, comfortably winning 3-0. The locals weren't so mouthy after that!

Burnley had an attractive draw for the FA Cup 3rd Round, at home to Liverpool, the Division One leaders at the time. I left Bromsgrove on the Friday afternoon, spent the night at my parents' home in North Wales and then borrowed my dad's car for the trip to Burnley. Les and I arrived pretty early and parked in Fulledge recreation ground. It was the time when we had a big open side where the Bob

Lord Stand would eventually be built and there were just panels alongside the construction site. Just as Les and I were sauntering alongside the ground, a coachload of Liverpool fans arrived and piled off the coach to attack us. Now I was 6 foot 2 and an ex rugby player but that is not a lot of good when you are confronted by over 30 aggressive Scousers! We managed to hot-foot it over to where some police officers were standing, but one of the Scousers managed to land a kick on my thigh. It was the only time I have been physically attacked by opposing fans (some Sunderland fans shouted "you fat bastard" at me in a motorway services place once, but that didn't hurt).
The cup tie ended 0-0 and we lost the replay. That wasn't important, as a return to the top division was our priority.

I managed to get up to Turf Moor (via North Wales again) to see a disappointing 1-0 defeat at the hands of Sheffield Wednesday but then I got lucky. Clive Stokes, my uncle (a proud Evertonian but a keen fan of any football), said that I could stay with them in Cwmbran over the weekend that Burnley were visiting Cardiff City. My uncle came with me to Ninian Park to witness an early Frank Casper goal which settled it. A good, professional victory and two more points towards promotion.

On the way home, my uncle asked me if I would set a good example to my younger cousin, who was showing an increasing fondness for booze. So I went to the local pub with cousin Fred and his mates, making sure that I set a good example by leaving before closing time. As I arrived back at uncle Clive's place, I tripped over the doormat and fell flat on my face. Hardly the best example to set!

I didn't get back to Turf Moor before promotion was confirmed when FA Cup finalists Sunderland were beaten.

I heard the news on the radio in Bromsgrove and, although it had been a foregone conclusion for some time, it was a wonderful feeling.

I saw two more home games that season, both 3-0 victories, against Brighton and Luton. I remember the Luton game as the first time I saw young Ray Hankin. So, promotion had been achieved but we still wanted to win the title.

The final game of that wonderful season was at Deepdale, the home of Preston North End. Although we had experienced an outstanding season, we still needed a point from that last game to be crowned Champions. Our close rivals, Queen's Park Rangers had also had a wonderful season and pushed us right to the wire. I borrowed my dad's car so Les and I made the trip up to what we hoped would be a Champions' party. As we got closer to the ground, there was claret and blue everywhere, making for a lively pre-match atmosphere.

This was the last time I saw Les Williams at a Burnley match until 2016 at Charlton – ironically another championship-winning performance.

Preston needed a point to avoid relegation and were in no mood to roll over. Just before half-time, Preston scored and we worried that they were going to be party poopers. But then Colin Waldron scored a memorable goal and we cruised along, as both sides got the point they needed. We were Champions, having played some really attractive football, and we had a young but talented side. Adamson's "Team Of The Seventies" were back in the big time!

Football League Division 2 : 1972-73		P	W	D	L	Pts
1.	Burnley	42	24	14	4	62
2.	Queen's Park Rangers	42	24	13	5	61
3.	Aston Villa	42	18	14	10	50
4.	Middlesbrough	42	17	13	12	47

The month after the Preston game, I finished my first college session in Bromsgrove and moved to Hotpoint's head office in Peterborough. As a skint student, and without access to my dad's car any more, I recognised that getting to Burnley games from my new base would be quite a challenge. Then something happened which meant that Burnley Football Club was no longer the most important thing in my life (and it still isn't)!

CHAPTER 5

KID IN A SWEET SHOP

"I never comment on referees, and I'm not going to break the habit of a lifetime for that prat." (Ron Atkinson)

"We didn't underestimate them, they were a lot better than we thought." (Bobby Robson)

When I lived in North Wales, I was over 50 miles away from the nearest league club and even further away from the nearest Division One clubs. The main North Wales coast road wasn't upgraded until after I left the area so travelling to matches was something of a challenge.

I mentioned that I had been engaged by Hotpoint as a trainee cost accountant, mixing hands-on practical experience with academic studies. So I was required to spend 6 months at college, followed by 6 months back in industry, and so on. There were apparently only 2 colleges in the country offering the specialist course I needed, and it was decided that I should study at Bromsgrove.

I lodged in the town, although hardly any of the other students on my course lived locally. In the evenings and at the weekends I was pretty much on my own. So, I spent many hours watching football, as Bromsgrove was only a short bus ride from Aston Villa, Birmingham City, West Bromwich Albion and Wolverhampton Wanderers. Villa and Birmingham were reached using the normal Midland Red buses but the Albion and Wolves matches required the use of "football special" buses from Bromsgrove. Between January and April I saw 15 games, not including the Burnley games.

Notts County

The first match I saw after moving to Bromsgrove was actually at Meadow Lane, where I saw Notts County beaten 4-1 by their visitors, Oldham Athletic. I was particularly impressed by Oldham's striker, David Shaw (who joined West Bromwich later in the season) – but the individual who really inspired me was the Meadow Lane disc-jockey. I don't know who he was but he deserved his own radio show – really humorous record dedications, sarcastic comments and he cut one record short as he was "fed up with that one now". Like a breath of fresh air and so unlike most football ground DJs and announcers.

I was actually in Nottingham for Rob Gawne's 21st birthday celebration. My other mate, Gwynedd Thomas, shared a house in West Bridgford, very near to the two Nottingham football grounds.

Birmingham City

The Blues had a decent side in the 1972-73 season, boasting the likes of Trevor Francis, Bob Latchford and John Roberts. The first time I saw them, they beat the reigning champions, Derby County, by 2-0. A 1-0 defeat to a Dougan-inspired Wolves stalled them a little, but 2-1 victories over Liverpool and Leeds ensured that they finished the season very impressively. It was before the Birmingham v Liverpool game that I experienced the worst crush at any match – really frightening for a few minutes, until an additional turnstile was opened.

My landlady's son-in-law was a Blues season ticket holder and he asked me to join 3 Blues fans for the away trip to Leicester at the end of the season. We arrived extremely early and spent too long in the pub, which meant we had to go several times through the packed crowd to the loo. At least I didn't miss the only goal of the game, scored by Alan Campbell.

The worst part about watching Birmingham City was having to put up with regular renditions of "Keep Right On To The End Of The Road".

West Bromwich Albion

The Baggies were not a great side in 1972-73, eventually getting relegated – and yet I never saw them lose at home. My first visit to The Hawthorns saw West Brom beat a decent Arsenal side 1-0, in an evening match. I stood near the Arsenal fans, who got in trouble with the local bobbies for singing

> *"Arsenal here, Arsenal there,*
> *Arsenal every f***ing where,*
> *la, la, la-la, la, la-la, la, la".*

Following their scolding from the police, they quickly changed it to

> *"Arsenal here, Arsenal there,*
> *we are not allowed to swear,*
> *la, la, la-la, la, la-la, la, la".*

I saw West Brom draw games against Southampton and Leeds, before an impressive 4-1 victory over Everton. One of my best mates at Bromsgrove, Greg Hands, was a Baggies fan and he drove me to the Everton game. He told me that he had kept wicket to Imran Khan during the previous summer, which really stung his hands.

I quite liked the Baggies fans, and I was sad to see them go down. They have usually brought a big following to Burnley over the years – a proper club with good fans.

Wolverhampton Wanderers

When I first started supporting Burnley, I was very much against Wolves because they were Burnley's big rivals. I mellowed over the years and I came to regard them as another well-established, well-supported club.

I discovered that a small bus went from Bromsgrove up to Molineux for all home matches, so I got myself involved. The first game I saw at Wolves was a 1-1 draw against Newcastle. It was the time of The Strawbs hit single "Part Of The Union" and the Wolves fans changed the words to:-

> *"I'm a Wanderers fan*
> *Amazed at what I am*
> *I say what I think*
> *That the Albion stink*
> *Yes, I'm a Wanderers fan"*

At that game I was able to compare the attributes of two potential England strikers, John Richards of Wolves and Malcolm Macdonald of Newcastle.

My next trip to Molineux saw Manchester City thrashed 5-1 and then I caught the Black Country derby game which saw Wolves beat West Brom 2-0. Wolves were an attractive side to watch, with the dangerous Dave Wagstaff putting in some excellent crosses.

Aston Villa

In 1972-73 the Villa were in Division Two, as were Burnley, and the only game I saw at Villa Park that season was the thrashing handed out by Burnley.

I shared a Midland Red bus back to Bromsgrove one night with a load of Villa fans. They entertained us with their version of when Birmingham City met Old Macdonald.

"Old Fred Goodwin had a farm
E I E I O
And on that farm he had some pigs
E I E I O
With a Francis here, and a Hatton there
Here a Page, there a Hynd
Everywhere a Latchford
Old Fred Goodwin had some pigs
E I E I O"

During the following season, 1973-74, I went to Villa Park twice to watch FA Cup matches. The first saw Aston Villa (still a Second Division side) beat Arsenal 2-0 in a replay. The second game was a replayed FA Cup semi-final between Liverpool and Leicester City. Bill Shankly's men came out on top, 3-1. Leicester would go on to lose the FA Cup Third Place match to Burnley, who had lost the other semi-final.

CHAPTER 6

TEAM OF THE SEVENTIES (Part 2)

"Football is a simple game; 22 men chase a ball for 90 minutes and at the end, the Germans win." (Gary Lineker)

"Dilly ding dilly dong" (Claudio Ranieri)

On 4th June 1973, I started working in my new department at Hotpoint's Peterborough HQ. On 10th July, I had my first date with one of my new colleagues, Diana. On 21st September we were engaged. I was 20, with no plans whatsoever to get into a steady relationship, let alone get engaged. But I was smitten and getting engaged was the best decision of my life.

Coping Well in Division One

It was really exciting to get a new set of fixtures with top clubs to face again – if perhaps a little frightening. If I assumed that the new love of my life would in some way prevent me from seeing Burnley, I was wrong, as she came with me to three games before my return to Bromsgrove.
Our first game in the 1973-74 season was away at Bramall Lane, the home of Sheffield United. Diana arranged for us to stay for the weekend with her aunty and uncle near Chesterfield, and then go to the match on the Saturday afternoon. Burnley were excellent, winning the game 2-0. The only downside was a serious injury to Mick Docherty. We returned to Derbyshire and had a wonderful evening in the local hostelries. That was my first experience of Derbyshire people, amongst the friendliest I have met. Before getting engaged, I thought I had better take Diana to meet her prospective in-laws, so we spent a weekend in North Wales in mid September – which coincided with a Burnley home match. So, my mother and fiancée-to-be joined me on the Bee Hole End terraces to see Burnley draw 1-1 with Derby County. Thankfully it was dry. Diana came with me by train from Peterborough to Leicester in November 1973 to see the Clarets beaten 2-0. It wasn't our best performance, but Leicester were decent that day.

Burnley did well in the first season after promotion, never really challenging for the title, but never out of the top 6. We combined this impressive league performance with a good FA Cup run, reaching the semi-final. I remember listening to the radio commentary of the match on a small transistor radio in Peterborough's main shopping area. And I remember the disappointment as Malcolm Macdonald twice outpaced the Burnley defence to score.

I returned to Bromsgrove at the end of November 1973 to continue my studies, but I spent every weekend in Peterborough as my in-laws-to-be very kindly allowed me to stay there. As I was away in Bromsgrove during the week, the priority for me was to spend as much time as I could at the weekend with my new fiancée. As a result, I didn't get to see Burnley again that season after the Leicester game.

As we had a successful season, Burnley were quite often on the television, so I was able to catch the odd glimpse. And a growing number of our players were starting to get international recognition (James, Dobson, Stevenson).

I managed to catch the opening game of the 1974-75 season against Wolves, as we were again staying with my parents for a few days. So, once more, my mother and my fiancée joined me at Turf Moor – this time in the comfort of the new Bob Lord stand. The result was a disappointing 2-1 defeat. And that was the only time I saw Burnley that season – a season which would see us flirting with the top positions, although we ultimately finished in tenth spot.

Two highlights of the season for me were my trips to Wembley (on a Hotpoint bus) to see England beat Czechoslovakia 3-0 and beat the reigning World Champions, West Germany, 2-0.

On March 1st, 1975, Burnley's 3-0 defeat of Coventry was featured on "Match Of The Day" and the impressive performance put us in second place, with a realistic chance of landing the title. And that was the pinnacle for Adamson's "Team Of The Seventies", as we only won one of our last ten games. The season had fizzled out badly, but worse was to come.

Down, Down, Deeper And Down

Diana and I were married in July 1975 and, unlike many of the newlyweds we knew, we threw everything we had into buying our own house in Peterborough. This meant that there wasn't much left for other material possessions, or holidays – and certainly not for a car. So, for three years we relied on local buses and lifts to get around. And it was out of the question to get up to Burnley, so I had to resign myself to the life of a remote (and sometimes distant) fan.

I didn't get to any Burnley matches in 1975-76 or in 1976-77, both of which were miserable seasons. We started in August 1975 with only one win in our first ten games and we were struggling in the bottom three from November onwards. Five consecutive defeats either side of Christmas didn't help and we ended up second from bottom. Only three years after promotion, we were back in Division Two.

	Football League Division 1 : 1975-76					
		P	W	D	L	Pts
19.	Birmingham City	42	13	7	22	33
20.	Wolverhampton W.	42	10	10	22	30
21.	Burnley	42	9	10	23	28
22.	Sheffield United	42	6	10	26	22

The following season started just as badly, with only two wins from our first eleven games. We almost fell straight through the Second Division, constantly flirting with the lower reaches of the league table. Only a revival from the middle of March saved us as we climbed up to 16th.

The 1977-78 season started off even worse than the previous two seasons, with only one win in the first 14 games. We stayed at the bottom of the table until January but a 10 game unbeaten run between February and April kept us up, finishing in 11th position.
I only got to see one game in that season. I had changed job within Hotpoint and they asked me to attend a Computer Appreciation course in London, which meant staying at a hotel for two nights. Before leaving home, I checked the morning paper to see what football matches were on in London that night. I was delighted to see that the Clarets were due to play at Fulham, so that was my evening taken care of.
Burnley were awful that night, losing 4-1, but at least I was able to see Rob Higgins playing for Burnley. He became a friend in later years and I am so pleased that I managed to catch one of his first team appearances.

The 1978-79 season was good, compared to the previous three seasons. We were in the top half of the table almost all year, occasionally in the top five, and we were never threatened with relegation. The highlight was doing the double over Blackburn Rovers, but we didn't win any of our last eight games, which was ominous. I only saw one Burnley game that season, a poor 4-1 defeat at Luton. That was my first experience of Luton's strange away end.

The final season of the 1970s saw us suffer the same fate as the first season – relegation. Our first win did not arrive until the 17th game, by which time we were bottom of the table. After managing a few wins in mid-season, we finished up by failing to win any of our 16 final fixtures. It was a truly dismal season which saw us relegated to the Third Division for the first time in our history.

The only game I saw that season was right at the end, a deserved 3-1 defeat at Cambridge United. As I drove on the A14 towards Cambridge, I could see a ramshackle bus ahead of me, belching out dirty-looking fumes. Sure enough, as I got closer, I could see claret and blue scarves in the back window. At the end of such a poor season we could still fill a bus with loyal fans.

Football League Division 2 : 1979-80						
		P	W	D	L	Pts
19.	Bristol Rovers	42	11	13	18	35
20.	Fulham	42	11	7	24	29
21.	Burnley	42	6	15	21	27
22.	Charlton Athletic	42	6	10	26	22

So, the 1970s had ended and poor old Jimmy Adamson's prediction had not come true. The decade had started badly, gone well in the middle, and then gone downhill fast. Now we could only look forward to Third Division football.

CHAPTER 7

PETERBOROUGH UNITED

"At the end of the day, the Arsenal fans demand that we put eleven players out on the pitch." (Don Howe)

"I was surprised but I always say nothing surprises me in football." (Ade Akinbiyi)

The fortunes of Peterborough United had caught my eye a few times during the 1960s. At the end of the 1959-60 season, Gateshead failed to gain re-election to the Football League and they were replaced by Peterborough United, who had won the Midland League for a few seasons in a row. No new team had been elected into the league for a decade, so it was all exciting stuff.

The "new boys" started off well as they were soon heading the Fourth Division and scoring for fun. Their leading scorer got 52 goals as "The Posh" won the division and scored a record number of goals.

In 1965, Posh captured the nation's attention when coming from behind to beat Arsenal 2-1 in the FA Cup 4th Round – Northern Ireland's striker Derek Dougan scored one of the goals.

They then caught my eye for a different reason. Burnley were top of Division One during November 1965 and in the fifth round of the Football League Cup we were drawn away at Third Division Peterborough. The home side won 4-0, all of the goals coming in the second half.

At the end of the 1967-68 season, Posh were demoted to the Fourth Division because of "financial irregularities", instead of merely having points deducted.

So I had been aware of the Posh more or less since they joined the league, and I looked forward to seeing them once I knew that the city would be my new working base. My lodgings were within walking distance of the London Road ground, and the folks with whom I lodged were Posh fans.

Born Is The King Of London Road

Halfway through the 1972-73 season, Fourth Division Peterborough United changed their manager, appointing the charismatic Noel Cantwell to the role. Cantwell made some impressive signings during the close season and there was an air of expectancy about the place, especially as the fans had an easy chant which was inspired by a Christmas carol

> "Noel, Noel
> Noel, Noel
> Born is the king of London Road"

My first visit to see the Posh was a pre-season friendly in August 1973 against West Ham United. I went with about 6 work colleagues, including Diana, to see the visitors win 2-1. It was a particularly sunny day, but I am not sure my new girlfriend saw much of the game from the terraces, as she was only 5 foot and one inch – and still is!

Peterborough started the season well and were challenging for the top positions straight away. I saw most of their home games before I went back to Bromsgrove. Cantwell had built an effective team, with veteran midfielder Freddie Hill pulling the strings and strong centre back Chris Turner marshalling the defence. Early in 1974, Posh got a home draw in the FA Cup against Division One leaders, Leeds United. The visitors were far too strong and ran out 4-1 winners but my main memory was how the Leeds fans behind the goal, dismantled the wooden refreshment hut and passed the pieces down over their heads to the running track. Dirty Leeds!
As I was in the Peterborough area every weekend, I got to see quite a few of Posh's Saturday home games, although they actually clinched the title in a midweek game against Gillingham.

In the Summer of 1974, I completed my apprenticeship with Hotpoint and I was given a regular job in an accounting role. I negotiated a day release arrangement so

I could complete my studies without having to go back to Bromsgrove. I carried on lodging in Peterborough until we got married in July 1975. As a result, I watched almost all of Posh's home games in the 1974-75 season and that included Diana's worst memory of the place.

She came with me to see Peterborough play Blackburn Rovers and we took our places on the long, uncovered Glebe Road terrace. The game started off in sunshine but then we had a light shower, followed by an absolute downpour. Diana had only washed her long hair that morning and was so unhappy at getting soaked that she left the ground and met me later at the bus station. She only ever came to one more Peterborough match and that was in 1985, when our six year old daughter presented the Hotpoint-sponsored match ball.

When we got married, we bought a house in northern Peterborough, no longer walkable from the football ground but easy to reach by bus. We had no car and getting to Burnley was not going to be easy. So, I got a season ticket at Peterborough

In September 1976 I witnessed the best goal I have ever seen and it occurred during a Football League Cup match between Peterborough and Fulham. The visitors had made a habit of signing star players who had maybe gone a little way past their "sell by" dates – like Bobby Moore, Rodney Marsh and George Best. In the match at Peterborough, the spectators' jaws dropped as Best scored a wonder goal, which I will allow the local sports reporter to describe:-

"He produced his own particular sort of wizardry, in the 40th minute when, after receiving a pass from Rodney Marsh, he stepped on the ball, flicked it into the air and

volleyed it past Posh keeper Eric Steele from fully 25 yards".

Barnwell

After Noel Cantwell had left Peterborough (for the first time), he was replaced by his deputy, John Barnwell. Barney built a solid side (featuring the steady defender, Ian Ross) which missed out on promotion right at the death, as they only drew their last match 0-0 with champions, Wrexham.
Midway through that season, Posh were quite close to the promotion spots but the fans were clamouring for more fire power. Then at Christmas time the club announced they had signed a player just for the fans. His name was Trevor Anderson and the Peterborough Evening Telegraph announced the signing as *"Fans' Christmas Anderson"*. It sounds even cornier now than it did then!
After Barnwell's team just missed out on promotion, Chris Turner moved on and the team started the next term badly. Barnwell wasn't given the funding he wanted, so he left and the Posh were relegated to the Fourth Division.

Morris

The former Ipswich midfielder, Peter Morris, managed Peterborough for a while and two highlights I remember from that era are an FA Cup tie at Notts County and a home league match against Aldershot.
Apart from trips to Wembley, I have only ever travelled with Peterborough to four away fixtures and one was in January 1981 to Notts County of the Second Division. A friend and his wife said they were going and asked me to join them. Fourth Division Posh were equal to County all

over the park and won the game with a strike by Robbie Cooke.

Towards the end of 1981, Posh hosted Aldershot in a floodlit Fourth Division fixture. Little Micky Gynn was outstanding as Aldershot were beaten 7-1

Wile

After a very impressive career as a central defender with West Bromwich Albion, John Wile was appointed manager of Peterborough in 1983. As well as himself, he seemed intent on building a squad of "giants" with Trevor Slack, Neil Firm, Alan Waddle and a player who produced the most impressive debut I have ever seen – Ray Hankin. I had obviously known of Hankin's qualities since I first saw him as a teenager at Turf Moor in 1973. He had done the rounds with Leeds, Middlesbrough and others by the time he came to Peterborough in September 1983. After his signing, I told all the locals how good Ray was, but even I was surprised by his debut.

Early on in the first half a cross came over and Hankin met it with a header from the edge of the penalty area. The ball flew to the top corner, giving the goalkeeper no chance, and the crowd gasped. Ray led the line with great authority, holding up the ball and then bringing his young colleagues into play. He later scored a second goal as Torquay United were beaten 5-0. During that season, it was apparent that Hankin had lost some of his pace and frequently he put in late tackles which saw him taking early baths. Good player, though.

It was during Wile's reign that my daughter got to present the match ball on the centre spot to the referee, as Hotpoint were the sponsors. She loved the occasion.

One experience I had to endure at Peterborough was the visit of Burnley in September 1985 – in the Fourth

Division. Burnley were my "big team", and Peterborough were my "other team", and I really did not want to see them playing each other on level terms. The first game between the two was a 0-0 draw but it took Burnley a few seasons to get the better of Posh. It was strange for me standing at the other end of the ground, having been frisked as an away fan upon entering.

Son Of God

After trying Noel Cantwell (again), Mick Jones, Mark Lawrenson and Dave Booth, Peterborough United appointed their ex-player, Chris Turner as manager in January 1991.
A match my daughter remembers well was the visit of Cardiff City as the season came to a close. As the visitors trailed 3-0, their fans decided to invade the pitch. The police responded by sending dogs on and there was a very funny image of a Cardiff fan running furiously, but not moving, as the alsatian had his jacket in its mouth

I started off watching the Posh from the open Glebe Road terrace, quite near to the halfway line. It was a good view, but you got drenched when it rained. I graduated to the terraced enclosure, partially protected from the rain by the roof of the main stand. But when my elder daughter started going regularly, we stood behind the goal at the London Road end. Ceri would not only join in with the songs and chants, she would even start them off sometimes.

Within 4 months, Peterborough had gained promotion to the Third Division, clinching it with a 2-2 draw at Chesterfield. They had been 2-0 down but clawed their way back in the second half to regain their Third Division status after 12 years in the bottom tier. The Chesterfield game was one of the few Posh away games I have attended and it was a great atmosphere.

The following season, 1991-92, saw the Posh coping quite well, if not spectacularly, but then finished the season on a roll, eventually finishing in sixth place – the final play-off spot. After winning the play-off semi-final at Huddersfield, Posh played Stockport County at Wembley in a bid to reach Division Two for the first time in their history. I took Ceri with me, as she had been attending quite regularly over the previous couple of seasons. She still comments on what a wonderful day it was. Peterborough's Ken Charley opened the scoring in the second half, only for Stockport to equalise very late in the game. Charley then added a second in injury time to clinch promotion. The journey home up the A1 was great fun as we passed coachloads of very happy Posh fans. Later that evening the manager, Chris Turner, and captain, Mick Halsall, joined celebrating fans in Peterborough's Cathedral Square.

In 17 months, Turner had taken the Posh from the fourth to the second tier of English football, and in the local fanzine he was christened "Son Of God". He subsequently became Chairman and owner of the club, before selling his share to Barry Fry. He suffered poor health for some years and died at the early age of 64. There is now a statue of Chris just outside the main entrance to the ground.

Fry Out, Fry Out

Barry Fry's first match as a Football League manager saw his Barnet team lose 7-4 to Crewe and his second match was a 5-5 draw with Brentford in the Football League Cup. His attitude was "however many you score, we will score even more", which made for much entertainment and lots of fans tearing their hair out.

He loved wheeling and dealing in the transfer market, with some success it has to be said. His previous manager's job before he came to Peterborough was at Birmingham City, where Jasper Carrott said their playing staff under Fry was the same as the population of Belgium.

Managers will tell you that when a substitute is introduced it takes a few minutes for them to get used to the pace of the game and become fully effective – that is why most managers introduce subs one at a time. Barry Fry was the champion of triple substitutions, which usually caused more chaos for his own side than for the opposition.

My younger daughter, Amber, became a Posh fan during Fry's period in charge and I have to say he was an excellent front man at open days, joking with the kids and their parents. Amber was not a singer or chanter like her sister had been but she got to understand the game and enjoyed the days out.

The 1999-2000 promotion season was great fun, and it included my witnessing the best hat-trick I have ever seen. It was scored by Peterborough's David Farrell in a fourth tier play-off semi-final at home to Barnet. Farrell's first two goals were excellent strikes into the top corner from about 20 yards. His third was struck from about 20 yards inside the Barnet half, clearing the keeper and dipping safely under the bar. Posh won 3-0 and made it to the final.

I picked Amber up from school and we drove down the A1 in appalling conditions (very wet weather and usual Friday evening traffic), arriving at our Wembley seats about 5 minutes after kick-off. The wet conditions ensured that the match was not a classic but Peterborough's Andy Clarke scored the only goal of the game to ensure

promotion. Both of my daughters attended Wembley play-off finals with the Posh – and so far they are unbeaten!
I recall going to Mansfield for an FA Cup match in late 2000 with my younger daughter – but then my attendance at Peterborough matches dwindled as I spent more and more time watching Burnley.

Barry Fry was not universally popular amongst Posh fans and there were frequent chants of "Fry Out" before, during and after games. Some Posh fans told me an amusing tale, which involves a group of Burnley fans.

During a holiday on one of the Greek islands, a family of Peterborough fans got friendly with a family of Burnley fans. In the club during the evening, it was normal to summon people up the stage and everyone would chant the person's name as they made the walk – "DAY-VID, DAY-VID", "CAR-LEE, CAR-LEE" and so on.

When it was the turn of one of the Burnley folks to walk up to the stage, the Peterborough family whispered across, "tell them that your name is FryOut". So she walked up to the stage with the whole room bellowing "FRY OUT, FRY OUT".

Recent Times

In recent years, I have seen Burnley play at Peterborough a few times (a special moment was Keith Treacy's belter of a goal in 2011). Apart from Burnley games, my only other recent visit to London Road was in April 2022, when Blackburn Rovers were the opposition. Blackburn opened the scoring ten minutes from the end, but Posh then scored twice to take the points. I cheered as loudly as the regulars!

I have often attended business meetings at Posh's ground and I still know one or two of the employees there. One day, perhaps when I become too old and doddery to drive to Burnley, I may watch the Posh more often again. I live about 9 miles north of Peterborough, I still have a soft spot for the club and I wish them well.

CHAPTER 8

AWFUL EIGHTIES

"Football is a game of skill, we kicked them a bit and they kicked us a bit." (Graham Roberts)

"I've been consistent in patches this season." (Theo Walcott)

The 1980s was one of the most miserable decades in Burnley's history. Apart from one promotion and one trip to Wembley, we saw some of the worst performances and some of the most dire results, culminating in a famous day when we almost lost our league status.

At the beginning of the decade we had just been relegated to the Third Division for the first time in our history. I recall a radio interview with Bob Lord when he was asked "how will you fare in Division Three?" and he replied "I don't know, we have never been there before".

Without seriously looking like promotion contenders, we fared reasonably well in our first season in the Third, finishing in 8th place. The only game I caught was a 1-1 draw with Rotherham United, who included Ronnie Moore (the father of our player, Ian). This was my first visit to Turf Moor for over 6 years. We had recently moved house, cash was not exactly plentiful and our Austin Princess regularly developed faults – so my trips to Burnley were scarce at this time.

What Goes Up ….

The 1981-82 season started badly but it turned out to be memorable. After 8 games, we were in 22nd position and seemingly in for a long hard struggle against relegation. We lost 6 games by October 3rd, but we only lost 2 more games all season! Playing our returned hero, Martin Dobson, as a sweeper was a master stroke as we slowly but surely climbed the table to finish as champions. The first game I caught was a 1-1 draw with Millwall in February, by which time the Clarets were in 5th spot.

My next game was a midweek match at Lincoln City, who were also fighting for promotion. I arrived early and received a complimentary ticket from Assistant Manager, Frank Casper, so I got a really good seat. I then watched us get battered by Lincoln until Trevor Steven scored from just outside the penalty area in the 88th minute to scrape an undeserved draw.

I managed to coax my stuttering Princess all the way down to Southend for the memorable Friday night promotion clincher. A 4-1 victory was a very appropriate way to gain the top spot, so I treated myself to fish and chips in Bishop's Stortford on the way home.

.... Must Come Down

The 1982-83 season was memorable but ultimately very disappointing. We enjoyed two very good cup runs, which meant that we always had games in hand over other teams – but we then failed to win those games in hand.

We lost at Bolton in mid-January, a result which sent us second from bottom. During the week that followed, we played Tottenham Hotspur in a Football League Cup quarter final tie, having already dealt impressively with Middlesbrough, Coventry and Birmingham. The day before the match, the board sacked Brian Miller and Frank Casper was put in temporary charge until the end of the season. I listened to the match on the radio, scarcely believing what I was hearing, as Burnley won 4-1.

I had never seen Burnley play in a semi-final before so I got myself a ticket for the second leg of the tie against mighty Liverpool. We lost the first leg 3-0 so the second leg was always going to be a struggle. Even so, I drove up to Burnley with two Liverpool-supporting work colleagues. We won the game 1-0 and just as we arrived back in Peterborough the Princess decided its water pump wasn't going to work any more.

I got lucky two weeks later. A work trip found me having to stay overnight in Manchester on the very night that Burnley were playing Crystal Palace in an FA Cup replay.

Still dressed in my work suit, I stood on the Bee Hole End terrace as we beat Palace 1-0, via a twice-taken penalty. We subsequently drew with Sheffield Wednesday in the quarter final but got battered 5-0 in the replay.
So, two memorable cup runs but in a poor shape league-wise. I went with a Newcastle-supporting work colleague to see our home game with The Toon – thankfully we went in his car – and we saw the Clarets win 1-0, Terry Donovan scoring the only goal.
The following week, I made the short journey to Cambridge and saw us lose 2-0 ("Bloody rubbish, Casper" was the regular call from the bloke standing next to me – and he was right). We then proceeded to lose our next four games (including one at Ewood) and dropped to the bottom of the table. We lost a last-match decider at Crystal Palace to be relegated with Bolton and Rotherham – a really topsy-turvy season with some highs but, ultimately, demotion back to the Third.

"John Bond's Burnley"

We started the 1983-84 season with a new, high profile, manager – which meant that the media would change our name to "John Bond's Burnley".
Bond came in, he shuffled and changed the playing squad and he was a regular interviewee on the television. We were the most newsworthy team in the lower divisions and, to an extent, Bond's changes were starting to work, as Burnley flirted with the top six. But then disaster struck! One of the players brought in by Bond was Kevin Reeves, a classy striker who linked very effectively with our Northern Irish international, Billy Hamilton. Reeves was injured, having scored 12 goals in 20 matches, and never played for us again. Our season went downhill, we lost all of our last four games and we finished 12th.

At the end of the season, Bond left the club, to be replaced by his assistant, John Benson. Benson's season started badly and continued to get worse. We were never far from the relegation zone and the only game I saw, a poor 1-0 midweek home defeat to Billy Bremner's Doncaster, was dire. I had visited my parents in North Wales and treated myself to a trip to Turf Moor on the way home – what a disappointment. We subsequently went down to the Fourth Division for the first time. Things couldn't get any worse, could they?

Life In The Fourth

Another "celebrity", Martin Buchan, was appointed manager for the start of the 1985-86 season, but he only lasted a couple of months, to be replaced by Tommy Cavanagh and then by Brian Miller (again). We didn't exactly set the Fourth Division on fire, shuffling between 8th and 12th for much of the season, finishing in 14th spot. Ominously, we only won one of our last eight games. I only saw two games that year, the 0-0 draw at Peterborough and a limp 2-0 defeat at Northampton Town. That was my first visit to The Cobblers' three-sided ground, with a bit of cord separating the playing area from the cricket pitch.

The Football League decided that the 1986-87 season would be the first where the bottom club in the Fourth Division would be relegated to non-league football. From the turn of the year onwards, Burnley were in constant touch with the relegation candidates, and things just seemed to get worse as the nightmare unfolded. A victory against Rochdale raised our hopes, but then defeats by Cardiff and Scunthorpe deflated us. A win at home to Southend lifted us once more but in our final away game we lost 1-0 to Crewe – and that left us in bottom place with just the one game to go.

There were several permutations possible, depending upon the other results. Burnley needed Lincoln or Torquay to avoid winning but nothing less than victory by ourselves would be enough.

Football League Division 4 : Friday, 8th May 1987						
		P	W	D	L	Pts
20.	Rochdale	45	11	17	17	50
21.	Tranmere Rovers	46	11	17	18	50
22.	Lincoln City	45	12	12	21	48
23.	Torquay United	45	10	17	18	47
24.	Burnley	45	11	13	21	46

This brought us to the finale of the season and arguably the most important game in the history of Burnley FC. This will always be known as "The Orient Game".

CHAPTER 9

ORIENT GAME

"If you don't believe you can win, there is no point in getting out of bed at the end of the day." (Neville Southall)

"When you are 4-0 up, you should never lose 7-1." (Lawrie McMenemy)

I had a good friend, Griff Morris, who worked at Hotpoint's factory in North Wales and his wife had worked with my mother for a while. Most importantly, he was a Burnley fan and he used to get the Monday version of the Lancashire Evening Telegraph sent to him every week. After reading Keith McNee's report he would pop the paper in the company's internal mail system and I would get to keep in touch with what was happening at Turf Moor.

Throughout the 1986-87 season, the newspaper reports were suggesting more and more that storm clouds were forming, none worse than a 6-0 home defeat by Hereford. I have since spoken to fans who attended that game and the feeling was that it really had been Burnley's worst-ever performance.

As each week went by, our relegation rivals seemed to be picking up unexpected points and we just seemed to be going backwards. In the early months of 1987, my wife was expecting our second child and I was loathe to clear off to Burnley for a whole day in the circumstances. Anyway, Amber was born in late April and I knew that I just had to be at Turf Moor for the last game of the season, "The Orient Game".

I stuck about four scarves in the back window of the car and left ridiculously early, as I wanted to soak up as much of the local atmosphere as possible before the game. On the main BBC radio news, the main sports story was all about the original Football League member which might drop out of the league later in the day. I arrived in Burnley at about 11.30am and I went for a walk around the town, asking anyone and everyone in claret and blue what they thought of our chances. There were one or two optimists around, but the majority thought we would be relegated because:-

1. our recent form had been abysmal
2. our opponents, Orient, were in with a chance of the promotion play-offs
3. we are Burnley and we don't win crunch relegation-deciding matches

Some folks were suggesting that the bank would pull the plug if we were relegated, so we could have no club at all. I will always support Burnley no matter what division or league they are in – but the thought of having no club hit me hard. Surely my beloved Clarets could survive?

I waited by the Players' Entrance and I was comforted to see Leighton James arriving. A link to our glorious past, and still a good performer. The crowd was building and it was clear that the gate was going to be much higher than we had experienced for some time. I made my way through the turnstiles and up towards the Longside terrace. Then I bought myself a pie, purely because I might never be able to do so again. The crowd grew, the noise went up a couple of notches and then the tension got a whole lot worse when the referee took the players off and delayed the start so that everyone could get in. The official crowd was just under 16,000 but it felt like more than that inside.

I didn't know until afterwards that the BBC had chosen our game for their live commentary that day. So, Burnley's survival attempt was deemed to be the most important and newsworthy game in the country. When the teams re-appeared, the noise was deafening and we prepared for the kick-off. I had never felt so tense and frightened before the start of a match – and I never have done since. It was as though we had all turned up to see a dear loved one for the last time and it was very emotional.

The first half of the game was pretty even. Orient had clearly come with a plan and they were not going to roll over. They were decent opponents.

Not long before half-time, Neil Grewcock cut in from the right and hit a left-footed shot into the far corner. A memorable goal which was just what we needed. Not long after the break, Burnley got another. Just about the smallest player on the pitch, Ian Britton, scored from a header and now we could sense some breathing space. Just before the hour mark, Orient threatened to spoil the party as they made it 2-1, a well taken goal by Alan Comfort. I understand that Comfort became a man of the cloth after leaving Orient, which is appropriate as many prayers were said at Turf Moor that afternoon.

The final thirty minutes of that game were absolute hell. We held our breath as every corner, free kick and throw-in were angled into our six yard box – and every lumped clearance was greeted with relief.

As news of other games filtered through, it became clear that we would stay up if we could hang on to our lead. The tension was unbearable, not helped by the fact we had "Teflon Joe" Neenan between the sticks.

Eventually the final whistle blew and the relief was enormous. Burnley had survived and Lincoln City had been relegated. For only the second time in my life, I went onto the hallowed pitch at Turf Moor, as everyone else seemed to do. Quite frankly, I was shaking with relief. I can only describe the feeling as if you had gone to bury a loved one, only for them to get up and walk away. The Clarets had lived to fight another day.

At the end of the game, the wonderful Orient fans applauded the Burnley fans – even though they had failed to reach the play-offs themselves. On my way home I was overtaken by a car containing Orient fans, who wound down their windows, gave me a thumbs up and then applauded me! Smashing club, smashing fans.

I bought almost every Sunday paper the following day and every one had the same headlines. Burnley's survival was big news. From the directors, manager and players came the same message – this must never be allowed to happen again.

Football League Division 4 : 1986-87						
		P	W	D	L	Pts
21.	Rochdale	46	11	17	18	50
22.	Burnley	46	12	13	21	49
23.	Torquay United	46	10	18	18	48
24.	Lincoln City	46	12	12	22	48

For years afterwards, fans of other clubs told me where they had been when Burnley survived the drop. Orient on 9th May 1987 will always be remembered as the most emotional game played by Burnley and it will be an experience I shall never forget.

CHAPTER 10

WEMBLEY (SHERPA VAN)

"Somebody compared him to Billy McNeill, but I don't remember Billy being crap." (Tommy Docherty)

"Certain people are for me and certain people are pro me." (Terry Venables)

The season after the "Orient Game" was comfortable enough, as Burnley hovered in the top half of the table for most of the season, eventually finishing 10th. It was nice not to be scrutinising the relegation zone, although we knew that another bad run could leave us looking over our shoulders again. The worst experience of my season was an embarrassing 5-0 defeat at Peterborough. You can imagine the teasing I received at the hands of my work colleagues on the Monday morning.

As well as playing our league fixtures, we played one FA Cup tie and a few League Cup matches. We also entered a tournament called the Sherpa Van Trophy, which was for Third and Fourth Division clubs. This tournament involved several early rounds, organised regionally, with a two-legged regional final and then a grand final at Wembley. Attendances at the earlier games are traditionally low but they pick up as clubs sense a Wembley final getting nearer.

Burnley's campaign started in October 1987, with a victory at Tranmere Rovers. That success was followed by wins over Rochdale, Chester, Bury and Halifax (the last one was won on penalties). We were then faced with a two-legged Northern Final against neighbouring Preston North End. So, two original members of the Football League fighting for a Wembley showdown against another original member, Wolves.

The prospect of a Wembley final really brought the crowds out – 15,500 for the first leg at Turf Moor and 17,500 for the second leg at Deepdale. The first leg finished 0-0, so North End probably thought they were favourites in the second leg, as they had home ground advantage. But goals by George Oghani, Ashley Hoskin and Paul Comstive gave visitors Burnley a 3-1 victory, and a trip to Wembley!

The Journey

My wife got hold of some claret and blue ribbons to affix to my car aerial and I covered the parcel shelf in a variety of Burnley scarves. Travelling down the A1, the first claret and blue car I saw was between Biggleswade and Stevenage, then I saw a couple of gold and black (Wolves) cars soon after. I was pleased that our opponents were Wolves. We had long been rivals, they had just won the Fourth Division title and I knew they would bring lots of fans with them to Wembley.

I arrived at Wembley very early, although a lot of fans were already there. The atmosphere was really convivial, with Burnley and Wolves fans mixing freely. I bought myself a programme and found my seat. I looked around the stadium, watched as the seats filled with fans and thanked my lucky stars. Only 12 months after clinging on to our league status, here we were at Wembley!

There was an ex-players match before the main event and the friendly family ambience continued.

The Match

The final was a relatively easy 2-0 victory for Wolves, who were the better side. It was nice that Leighton James made an appearance from the subs bench, the team had performed satisfactorily and the result didn't matter.

The Aftermath

Nearly 81,000 people had seen two Fourth Division teams battle it out at Wembley.
The occasion was a kind of reward for putting up with some of the rubbish which had gone before, and it was a great day out.
As I was leaving the car park, a set of Burnley fans were organising an impromptu match with some Wolves fans – the losers were to buy the beer on the way home! I stopped at a Little Chef on the A1 and met a family of Wolves fans from East Anglia, who had clearly had a good time.

In 1984, my job with Hotpoint changed substantially. I became responsible for Hotpoint's export business, and this involved me in a lot of international travel. I was keen to climb the corporate ladder and I recognised that the only way to achieve that was by working my socks off. By the time of the 1988 Sherpa Van final, my travelling was really starting to ramp up and I had two daughters who didn't see as much of their dad as they should. I decided to end my cricket career and I recognised that my trips to Burnley matches would not be as frequent as I would like.

Arsenal

One match I did manage to attend in this period was on 2nd January 1989, when Arsenal beat Spurs, 2-0. My dad had supported Arsenal since the early 1930s but he had never been to Highbury. I found out that Arsenal had a home game during the weekend that my parents would be staying with us so, during a business trip to London, I bought two tickets for the North London derby game. Dad didn't know we were going until the day before the game. I drove to Cockfosters and then we tubed it into Highbury.

I bought him a scarf and we took up our seats in the famous old stadium. The game was entertaining and one of my dad's favourite players, Paul Davies, scored one of the goals in a 2-0 win over their arch rivals. My dad never went to an Arsenal home game again and I am very glad that I got that chance to take him.

Out With A Whimper

The 1988-89 season started off with 3 straight wins, including a 6-0 thrashing of York City, which put us in first place temporarily. We then drifted into mid-table mediocrity and did the same the following year.

The 80s had begun badly with relegation from the Second Division, had promised much after the 81-82 promotion campaign, then dived dramatically to the depths of the "Orient Game". The rest of the decade then just seemed to fizzle out.

I saw no Burnley league games during those last three seasons in the 80s, keeping in touch mainly via the teletext services Ceefax and Oracle. They used to take ages to come around to the page you wanted – and you daren't leave the room in case you missed your page!

The new decade started better, as Burnley challenged for a play-off place pretty much throughout the 1990-91 season. We finished in 6th place but then missed out on promotion when losing the two-legged play-off semi-final to Torquay United. The home game against Torquay was the time that Blackburn fans flew over Turf Moor with a nice kind message for us.

Good riddance to the "Awful Eighties".

CHAPTER 11

WEMBLEY (PROMOTION 1)

"Germany are a very difficult team to play. They had eleven internationals out there today." (Steve Lomas)

"Oh, he had an eternity to play that ball, but he took too long about it." (Martin Tyler)

Frank Casper had been in charge since early 1989 and he must have been fairly happy with the 6th place finish at the end of the 1990-91 season. If we could get off to a good start to the following season, we just might get an automatic promotion spot and not have to worry about the play-offs. Casper had a terrible September, losing three consecutive games, and his assistant, Jimmy Mullen, took over the reins.

Jimmy Mullen's Claret And Blue Army

It is always nice to start off in a new manager's job with a victory. Jimmy Mullen started off with NINE straight victories, and I saw the ninth of these wins at Northampton. On-loan keeper Andy Marriott played his last game for us as the Clarets took an early lead. The Cobblers equalised with five minutes to go, only for top scorer, Mike Conroy, to get the winner a minute later.

Burnley hit the top of the table and stayed there until the end of the season. Promotion was clinched in a famous away victory at York, with "Super" John Francis getting a late winner to confirm the three points. I heard the result on a radio in Northern France, where I was just able to pick up BBC Radio 4's news programme.

	Football League Division 4 : 1991-92					
		P	W	D	L	Pts
1.	Burnley	46	25	8	9	83
2.	Rotherham United	46	22	11	9	77
3.	Mansfield Town	46	23	8	11	77
4.	Blackpool	46	22	10	10	76

Our first season up after promotion went well, with Burnley floating either side of halfway and never in much trouble. Adrian Heath starred up front, still a class act.

We started well in the 1993-94 season, establishing ourselves in the top 8. I managed to see this promising side in a League Cup replay at Tottenham. We did not disgrace ourselves in a 3-1 defeat, with Adrian Heath, Kevin "Rooster" Russell and David Eyres posing quite an attacking threat. Burnley stayed in the play-off zone for the whole season and I managed to get up to Turf Moor in early April to see Tony Philliskirk get a hat-trick in a 5-0 hammering of Barnet.

The Play-Offs

Sure enough, Burnley finished in the final play-off spot of 6th and our opponents in the play-off semi-final were Plymouth Argyle. I attended the first leg at Turf Moor, which was a disappointing 0-0 draw – and I thought we had blown our chance. I listened to the second leg on the radio and was elated when "Super" John Francis broke away twice to put us 2-1 in front. Warren Joyce added a third and then, to quote the radio commentator "Jimmy Mullen's claret and blue armada set sail from Plymouth, bound for Wembley and the Promised Land".

I was tied up with exhibitions when the tickets went on sale and left things a little late. And then, when I drove up, I got a puncture near Wakefield so got to Burnley later than I had planned. When I got to the window I was told that the only tickets left were the cheap ones (low down near the front) or up in the Olympic Gallery – but they were going to cost £32. Quite frankly, I would have given a thousand and thirty two pounds to see Burnley in a play-off final, so I left Turf Moor with my precious ticket.

The pre-match build-up included the production of a special song (which I still have on my phone) and much speculation about Burnley's chances of beating Stockport County, who had finished 12 points ahead of us in the regular league campaign.

Twin Towers

When I arrived at Wembley after driving down. I stood at the top of Wembley Way and marvelled at the number of claret and blue buses arriving. We substantially outnumbered the Stockport fans and the atmosphere was wonderful. I climbed up to my seat in the Olympic Gallery and awaited the teams.

The game got off to a terrible start when Stockport took a very early lead. Then Ted McMinn played his party piece, by annoying a defender so much that the defender retaliated and got himself sent off.

An excellent David Eyres goal levelled up the game at 1-1 and then a second Stockport player got sent off. Our winner was scored by Gary Parkinson, a player who remains much-loved by Burnley and Middlesbrough fans as he copes bravely with his terrible illness.

Being at Wembley to see Burnley lift the play-off trophy was a wonderful experience. Seven years after the "Orient" nightmare, we were headed for the second tier.

We did not start too well in what was called the First Division, failing to win our first five games. The first game I saw that season was away at Millwall, an evening game during which I worried about seeing my car again.

We aggravated the locals by winning 3-2 but I didn't see any trouble.

My travels ensured that I didn't see many Clarets games, relying instead on teletext and radio reports.

We were never far from relegation worries and then I saw two contrasting matches during January 1995. The first was a surprising 4-2 victory at Cambridge in the FA Cup, followed by a dismal 3-0 league defeat at Notts County.

At the Notts County game, I took my place in the away end very early and I watched the seats filling up. About six or seven rows in front of me were a couple (perhaps in their thirties) and a lady who looked very much like one of their mothers. As soon as the teams came out, these three folks moved pretty sharpish. Behind them was seated Derek "Rocky" Mills, one of the loudest, most aggressive, most foul-mouthed and famous of all Burnley fans. I think he had only bellowed out "Who are ya?" a few times when the folks moved, he saved the profanities for later.

We started 1995 with 8 straight league defeats and things were looking pretty grim by the time we got into March.

And then I made some new friends!

CHAPTER 12

DUBLIN CLARETS

"Wilkins sends an inch-perfect pass to no-one in particular." (Bryon Butler)

"Hodge scored for Forest after 22 seconds ... totally against the run of play." (Peter Lorenzo)

When I took over Hotpoint's exports, I quickly recognised that our potential in the Republic of Ireland was nowhere near being realised. I therefore put in a substantial stint over a number of years to grow that piece of business from £1 million per annum up to £16 million. This wasn't just due to me, of course. My distributor's staff, in addition to my own service and training colleagues, all made a prodigious effort to ensure our progress.

One of the reasons for our success was the fact that I regularly visited Ireland, to understand the people and the market dynamics. I went to Ireland just about every month for 11 years and I developed firm friendships as well as sound business relationships.

One Friday evening in early 1995 I sat on my plane home and chose the local newspaper to read, rather than a British paper. As my dad had taught me, I started to read the paper on the sports pages first – and an advertisement caught my eye. A meeting of the "Dublin Clarets" was advertised, for all Burnley fans in Ireland, to take place at the Trinity Inn on Pearse Street. And the date coincided with my next visit to Dublin!

The contact was Sean Coleman and over the weekend I telephoned him to ask him about the group and to see whether a visitor could pop along to the meeting. Seemingly, the Dublin Clarets group was the result of a chance meeting at Stansted airport following the promotion play-off final at the end of the previous season. They each recognised the claret and blue shirts and scarves, so they got talking and decided to organise regular get-togethers for any Clarets fans in or around Dublin. So, by the time I made contact with Sean, the group had been operating for 9 or 10 months. They met every month and occasionally would travel together to Turf Moor.

Sean was very positive and made it clear that I would be more than welcome at any of their meetings. So, I turned up at the Trinity Inn for the next meeting and gradually about 6 or 7 guys in Burnley shirts filtered in. The Guinness flowed during the evening and I was able to experience how well-informed, optimistic and passionate the Dublin lads were.

I attended a number of boozy Dublin Clarets meetings until I stopped travelling to Ireland but I often bumped into them at Turf Moor thereafter. Whenever I visited Dublin after a trip to Turf Moor, I would be interrogated in minute detail as to the performance of the team and the individual players – as though my opinion was more valid than the official reports. Woe betide me if I hadn't noticed how the left back and left winger combined together! And, of course, I was able to give them programmes, fanzines etc.

I got to know Sean and his two brothers, Gerry McKinney, Graham Verso and Hughie the ref. I have it easy compared to the Irish lads. For them to travel to Turf Moor involves either a ferry or a flight – and then they have to get to Burnley after they have landed in the UK. They give up an awful lot of time and money to support Burnley and their loyalty is to be admired.

I was an "honorary" Dublin Claret for a while and I thank them for their friendship. They also introduced me to someone who has done more than anyone to help me to support Burnley. I asked the Dublin group how they were able to get tickets for home and away games and the reply was "We get Allen to help us. You must know Allen. Everyone knows Allen".

Well, I didn't know who Allen was, but I was about to. The Dublin lads suggested that I should contact him because he went out of his way to help remote Burnley fans.

CHAPTER 13

ALLEN RYCROFT

"I've had 14 bookings this season, 8 of which were my fault – but 7 of which were disputable." (Paul Gascoigne)

"I think that France, Germany, Spain, Holland and England will join Brazil in the semi-finals." (Pele)

I took the advice of the Dublin Clarets and made contact with Allen Rycroft. Allen was born and bred in Burnley, living a short distance from Turf Moor. His father had taken him to watch Burnley play as a child and he remained a Clarets fan throughout his teens and into adulthood.

Allen had attended every type of Burnley game over the years – first team, reserves, youth team – home and away. He was well known to the players, often giving them lifts back after matches, and he often did jobs in and around Turf Moor, using the apprentice players as his army of workers. For a while Allen's sister worked in the Turf Moor ticket office. So, when it came to acquiring tickets, meeting players (former and current) or attending functions, there was no better contact than Allen.

He recognised that it was extremely difficult for non-local fans to queue up for big match tickets, so he took it upon himself to make it easier for us remote fans to support the Clarets. He would get tickets, collect people from airports, put them up at his home and provide a full English breakfast the following morning. Nothing was too much trouble for him, he just wanted to make the supporting of Burnley an easy and pleasant experience.

When I first spoke to Allen, he explained that he attended almost all Burnley away games and that I would be welcome to join him if his route was remotely in my region. Coincidentally Allen and his mate, Cliff, were planning to attend the away match at Southend the following Saturday (that would be 8th April, 1995). So, it was agreed that they would pick me up at Norman Cross on the A1 and then we could watch the game together. We arrived at Southend in good time and even had time for some fresh air down by the sea. When we arrived at the ground we didn't head for the normal turnstiles, instead we were to collect our tickets from a special desk.

Allen had warned me to wear a jacket and tie for the game, but I didn't realise that we would be sitting with the directors and dignitaries. Allen knew most of the directors at the time (Frank Teasdale, Clive Holt, Bernard Rothwell) but he was particularly friendly with Bob Blakeborough. Throughout the rest of this book I will mention a number of grounds I have visited and in many cases my tickets (and passes to lounges) were arranged for me by Allen and Bob.

At Southend we watched a poor 3-1 defeat, which dropped us further into the relegation mire. I enjoyed the journey home, though, as I discovered how learned Allen was on all matters surrounding Burnley. I won't mention the speed at which Allen drove, in case any members of the Cambridgeshire Constabulary read this book!

Myself and five of the Dublin Clarets once spent the night on Allen's floor after (a) watching a relegation crunch match and (b) quaffing large amounts of ale at the Queen Hotel, Holme Chapel. The following morning, Allen's wife at the time (Jeanette) served up breakfasts for all. Allen introduced me to a number of Burnley-supporting characters on our travels. One regular supporter at away games was just known as "Nigel from Dover" and he could be seen all over the place, hardly missing a game. On one occasion Allen arranged for the kit man to leave a ticket for me when we played at Peterborough. When I arrived there were actually two tickets, so I managed to find "Nigel from Dover" and let him have one of them.

Allen and I got into the sponsors' lounge at Leicester City on the day that Burnley became the first away team to win at Leicester's new stadium. Whilst in there, we met Gary Lineker and David Neilson, the Coronation Street actor (a Foxes fan).

I think the best story I can tell about Allen's generosity is the way in which I acquired a Play-Off Semi-Final second leg ticket at Reading. This was a sell-out game, and the winners would be going to Wembley. I had no opportunity to travel up to Burnley and queue for a ticket, so Rycroft said "don't worry, I will sort something". I got a ticket for one of the most memorable games I have seen because Allen Rycroft queued in the pouring rain for two hours, and he didn't even go to the game himself!

I have always told Allen that he has far too much hair for a man of his age, he bollocks me for paying too much for a bottle of coke and he is not exactly backward at coming forward. But he has gone out of his way to help me to be a Burnley fan and I am extremely grateful for his help and friendship.

CHAPTER 14

RE-SCHEDULING

"I couldn't settle in Italy. It was like living in a foreign country." (Ian Rush)

"Getting kicked in the shin is painful but it doesn't hurt." (Nuno Gomez)

Our first season down after relegation was not a happy one, as we tried three different managers and only finished six points clear of an unthinkable drop back into the dreaded fourth tier. I managed to see the Clarets winning 2-0 at Peterborough and I also enjoyed a visit to Old Trafford (and the impressive museum) to watch my second Manchester derby. This time City lost 1-0.

I got to Old Trafford again in November 1996, to watch United play Arsenal. The ticket and all the hospitality were paid for by one of our suppliers – they also took me to Edgbaston test matches a couple of times. The Arsenal defence were immaculate all through the game until a bodged back pass gave United the only goal of the game.

The 1996-97 season was much better for Burnley as Adrian Heath's side finished only five points off the play-offs. Unfortunately, I witnessed a 3-2 defeat at Peterborough that season and once again a new manager was appointed before the next campaign – the former England international, Chris Waddle.

The late nineties was my busiest period whilst in employment and I spent a lot of time abroad, I attended lots of meetings in and around London and I was often involved in taking overseas customers to our factories in North Wales, the South West and the Potteries. So, I had to be very clever and, wherever possible, re-schedule my work commitments so that I could catch the odd Burnley match.

In February 1998, I managed to change my incoming flight so that I landed at Heathrow three hours before Burnley kicked off at Wycombe Wanderers. I just about parked up in time to see us lose 2-1. On another occasion, a delayed flight into Stansted meant that I arrived at Colchester United's ground (Layer Road in those days) just as the teams were coming out. I was starving so I queued up for nearly ten minutes to get a pie or something – and while I was in the queue Burnley scored twice! We subsequently won 4-0, and that included a goal by the Norwegian, Rune Vindheim.

Once I managed to break my return journey from our factory near Bristol by popping in to watch our away game at Reading – a tedious 0-0 draw. Happily, a trip to our factory near Stoke enabled me to see a memorable 4-1 Burnley victory – a game which featured a goal by full-back, Ally Pickering, against his former club.

After one trip away, I arrived back at Heathrow on a Saturday morning and went to collect my car from the hotel car park I had used – only to find that my car was an absolute mess after all the local birds had used it as a toilet for three days. I received some strange looks from the locals as I left my car in the Sainsbury's car park adjacent to Crystal Palace's ground. The bird droppings must have been lucky for Burnley, as Graham Branch scored the game's only goal.

During my firm's new product exhibitions, I frequently had to stay in London for a few nights. One such stay coincided with Burnley's visit to Craven Cottage. Fulham had a decent side and beat us 3-1, but the balti pie was tasty!

I also managed to arrange work trips so that they coincided with Burnley away games at Watford, Birmingham City, Walsall and Stockport County. It often felt strange to be in work attire whilst everyone around me was in more usual clothes. On one occasion, I attended an evening match with Sir Vincent Fean, a Burnley lad who had a spectacularly successful career in the diplomatic field. Vincent arrived straight from work, dressed in a smart, charcoal suit, crisp white shirt, sober tie – and a very scruffy claret and blue bobble hat!

"Chris Waddle's Burnley" had a miserable season and were never clear of the relegation zone. Chris had been an outstanding player and he was still well worth his place in the team, but his record as a manager was poor.

We reached the final game of the 1997-98 season knowing that, to avoid relegation back to the fourth tier, we had to win our final match at home to Plymouth and hope that Brentford did not beat Bristol Rovers. I arranged to travel up to Turf Moor for the relegation decider and Allen Rycroft fixed it for me (and the Dublin Clarets) to attend a function at the Keirby Hotel on the Saturday evening. Two goals by Andy Cooke ensured that Burnley won the nervy game 2-1, Brentford lost in Bristol, and the Clarets had survived.

Whilst all Clarets fans were relieved to have escaped the drop back into the fourth tier, there was anger that we had found ourselves in a position where we might drop down. We wanted to be rid of relegation worry and concentrate on the top two divisions and not the bottom two. For that to happen there would have to be changes and before the next season Chris Waddle was replaced by Stan Ternent.

I was happy with that decision. Stan had a reputation for being a "no nonsense" manager and, if we were to climb the divisions, we needed to be prepared to roll up our sleeves and graft.

CHAPTER 15

RECOVERY UNDER STAN

"I would not be bothered if we lost every game as long as we won the league." (Mark Viduka)

"John Hartson's got more previous than Jack The Ripper." (Harry Redknapp)

Stan Ternent had played for Burnley in the 1960s and had an impressive pedigree as a coach and manager. However, because he was operating for much of his first season with players signed before he joined the club, things did not immediately go well. He sacked four players in his first month and made it clear that players did things his way, or they were out.

At the turn of the year Burnley were in 17th place, just above the danger area. But in the middle of February we went on a disastrous run which saw us lose four consecutive games, without scoring a goal! First we lost 2-0 at Wycombe Wanderers, followed by an embarrassing 5-0 home defeat to Gillingham (four of which came in the first half). Then, in front of over 17,000 fans, we were battered 6-0 at home to Manchester City. Our neighbours, Preston North End, joined the party by taking all three points from Turf Moor with a 1-0 victory. Burnley seemed to be unable to come back once we had gone behind. We were going downhill fast (down to 21st after the Preston defeat) and that would only end in the fourth tier.

One of the most significant turning points in Burnley's history took place on Saturday 20th March 1999 and I was able to witness that event.

The Turning Point

At the end of December 1998, my dad was taken into hospital and within a few days his ailment was identified as lung cancer (he had been a smoker since he was ten). We were told that he probably had three months to live. Wherever I happened to be with my work, from early January I travelled to North Wales every weekend and spent some time with my dad while I was still able to do so. One of my trips to North Wales coincided with

Burnley's visit to Wrexham, so I arranged to drop into The Racecourse on my way.

On the quarter hour, Wrexham opened the scoring and the mood amongst the crowd was that we wouldn't get back into the game and that would mean no points again. But this is where everything changed!
Burnley did fight back, Burnley did score a second half equaliser and Burnley did get a point from the game. After the Wrexham game, we still had ten games to play – and we didn't lose another game that season! We were two down against Macclesfield in our next game – but fought back to win a 4-3 thriller. The attitude had changed and the wonderful finish to the season ensured that we would start the following season on the front foot.

My dad died at the end of April 1999 and, during my last weekend with him, we watched Arsenal win 6-1 on "Match Of The Day", meaning that Arsenal were top of the league on the day he died. He'd have liked that!

Good-Bye To The Third Tier

Burnley started the 1999-2000 season well, winning three and drawing one of our first four games. We continued to impress and by December we were in the top four or five, looking good for at least a play-off spot. My first chance to see this team was at Premier League Derby in a third round FA Cup tie. As an experiment the third round was scheduled for completion before Christmas, so we played on the early date of 11th December. The Rams had only recently moved to Pride Park and I was lucky enough to see a famous Clarets victory (courtesy of a headed Andy Cooke goal) from the comfort of padded seats in the directors' box. We played very well against our Premier League opponents and Stan had us really bubbling!

A couple of weeks into the new year, I made the journey to Chesterfield and was fortunate again to get a ticket for the directors' box and pre-match lounge. I can honestly say that the welcome I received from the home club was the friendliest I have ever experienced. There was a never-ending supply of teas and coffees, plus the most delicious home-made food you could imagine. And the ladies who looked after us acted like our mothers! What a wonderful experience – and we got a handy 1-1 draw.

One day in mid-February I was walking between buildings at work when one of the local Posh fans called across to me **"Hey, Mike, have you heard? Burnley have signed Ian Wright!"** Like most people, I just didn't believe it – surely it was a wind up? But, as the day progressed, every football fan I knew at work was ringing me or messaging me to confirm the rumours. All of a sudden, Burnley were big news and the Wright signing made a big statement – Burnley were serious about their push for promotion and the effect on attendances was profound.

My first chance to see the Wright-inspired Clarets was the away match at Colchester on 26th February. Two goals from centre back Steve Davis were enough to secure a 2-1 victory, which kept us in 5th place. There was an air of excitement amongst the fans, as though we were really starting to go places.

We lost a couple of games after the Colchester match but then we embarked on a superb run until the end of the season, only losing one of our last thirteen games. March and April were particularly busy months for me at work, organising overseas trade shows and effectively doing three jobs, as we sought to replace departing colleagues. On the last day of the season, Burnley needed to win at

Scunthorpe, while Gillingham needed not to win at Wrexham, if we were to be promoted. But, rather than taking up my place on the terraces at Glanford Park, I was at premises in London near to the Millennium Dome (it became the O2 some time later) doing our last-minute rehearsals before a major product launch the following day. Just outside our main building were our AV team, checking all the sound and lighting – and, significantly, listening to Radio 5 Live.

I popped out as often as I dared to check on the scores at Scunthorpe and Wrexham. Things started well, as Wrexham took an early lead, but Scunthorpe then scored in our match. Micky Mellon equalised just before half-time and then Glenn Little scored what would prove to be our winner with about a quarter of an hour to play. Those last few minutes were unbearable as I crouched over that radio and willed us to hang on. The news from Wrexham was wonderful and my colleagues could tell what had happened when I re-joined them, grinning from ear to ear.

Wrighty didn't stay beyond the end of the season, but his masterful signing by Ternent had given the whole club a shot in the arm. From the "turning point" at Wrexham in March 1999 to the good news from Wrexham in May 2000, Stan Ternent had dragged us from near-relegation to automatic promotion alongside Preston North End. He had made changes along the way and he had demonstrated impressive motivational qualities. The cherry on the top was the way he used his reservoir of contacts to add Ian Wright to the group.

Burnley's two previous promotions to the second tier had resulted in our instant returns, being relegated after only one season. So, the big question was "Stan has got us up but can he keep us there?"

So Close

We needn't have doubted Stan! Burnley never did struggle at the higher level (apart from 5 consecutive defeats around Christmas) and we were in the top ten all season. I managed my work schedule to catch the early Crystal Palace and Fulham games, then made my way to Watford in late November for the match against the Hornets.
I arrived early, parked up and took my seat in the stand. By ten past two, the ground was starting to fill and we looked forward to seeing the teams going through their pre-match routines. Then the heavens opened and the ground was subjected to non-stop torrential rain for about half an hour. Even then, the rain didn't stop entirely, it continued to fall, though not so fiercely. The referee appeared, together with the ground staff and the two managers. A forlorn attempt was made to kick a ball a few yards, and the decision was made to postpone the game. Luckily, the match was rearranged for an evening in mid March, which coincided with a trip to Heathrow, so I was able to catch the game, stay overnight near the airport and then take my early morning flight the following day.

My first-ever Burnley-Blackburn derby game took place in mid December. I did not enjoy the occasion – the atmosphere was hostile, not helped by Kevin Ball's unforgettable tackle on David Dunn. Rovers handled the emotion better than we did, we lost 2-0 and I got diverted off the M1 on the way home. Misery!

After the turn of the year, I got to visit the coldest ground I've been to, Blundell Park – the home of Grimsby Town. The fish and chips outside the ground were delicious but that cold wind straight off the North Sea was horrible. And we lost, 1-0.

My next away game was at Norwich City, where I got introduced to their famous director, Delia Smith. The staff at Carrow Road were very friendly and it helped that the sun shone. We came from behind to win 3-2.

We stayed up with the pace and we only lost one of our final eight games – but we finished in seventh place, only two points away from the play-offs. It was a magnificent achievement by Stan Ternent to take a newly-promoted side so close to the play-offs in their first season up. But it got even better!

So Close Again

Burnley's start to the 2001-02 season was incredible, winning seven out of the first eight games to head the table and I saw the eighth of these games. I was lucky enough to arrange a work trip to North Wales to coincide with Burnley's visit to St. Andrews, the home of Birmingham City – who were a more than useful side. Their lightning-quick forward, Andy Johnson, caused us a few problems that night but we had Glenn Little, who was the best player outside the top division at that time. Little scored two and made one of our goals in a 3-2 victory. My next game after the Birmingham match was away at Norwich City. During the game, the scoreboard showed the scoreline Manchester United 1 Scum 0. After the game (and after the press had got hold of it), Norwich City offered an official apology to Ipswich Town – but I must say that we all saw the funny side.
Despite the odd blip (one of which I caught at Nottingham Forest) we kept up the pace and at Christmas we were well on top of the division, having just gone ten matches without defeat.

On 29th December we visited our nearest rivals, Manchester City, and that is where it all started to go wrong. I listened to the game on the radio and felt thoroughly sick at the end of the game, which ended in a 5-1 defeat. Perhaps it wasn't going to be so simple, after all.

We blew hot and cold for the rest of the season, although our superb start had guaranteed that we would be in the mix until the end. I caught our 1-0 defeat at Walsall and our 2-0 win at Stockport (a Saturday morning stocktake at our Manchester warehouse conveniently ensured I was in the right place at the right time). Disappointingly, we lost our penultimate game at relegation-threatened Grimsby, which meant that we had to win our last game of the season and hope that goal difference would work in our favour.

We knew that Norwich had won 2-0 so we had to better our 1-0 scoreline against Coventry to qualify for the play-offs. Our latest signing, England legend Paul Gascoigne, had two late free kicks saved by the visiting keeper and this meant that we had missed the play-offs by one goal!

Uwe, Uwe!

In the early part of 2002 I got the chance to actually put something back and do a favour for a Clarets legend. I found out that a Testimonial Dinner was being arranged to celebrate the long career of Brian Miller, a former player, coach and manager of the Clarets.

I used my business contacts in Germany to put me in touch with a Hamburg-based journalist, who very kindly conducted an interview on my behalf with former German skipper, Uwe Seeler. As well as sending good wishes to Brian, he shared his memories of the 1960-61 European

Cup tie between Burnley and Hamburg, then he signed a photograph.
I got Uwe's words and the signed photograph framed and I was able to present them to Brian at the dinner on 25th May 2002. It was a wonderful evening, graced by Burnley stars from 1960 to 2002, and I am just grateful that I got the chance to contribute.

Goals Galore

We started the 2002-03 season with four straight defeats. We ended up by conceding more goals than anyone else in our division and I saw these incredible games
>   Grimsby 6 Burnley 5
>   Burnley 4 Watford 7
>   Burnley 2 Sheffield Wednesday 7

Our defending in all of these games (and in ten other games where we conceded at least three goals) was appalling.

Just before the Grimsby debacle, I had the pleasure of going to Ipswich for an evening game. I arrived extremely early, parked up and made my way to the reception to collect my ticket for the directors' box (thanks again, Bob). I picked up my ticket and I was ushered into a special lounge, where I was greeted by a delightful lady named Pat Godbold, who had been a PA for Alf Ramsey and Bobby Robson in previous years. As the first Burnley person to arrive, Pat mothered me and made sure I helped myself to the food and drink. But she carried on looking after me right up until the match started. She knew everyone in the club and all players, officials and dignitaries made a beeline for her when they arrived.

And she insisted that I be introduced to everyone, including Russell Osman, Harry Redknapp and Kevin Bond. I managed to avoid her gaze at the end, as we had sneaked a 90th minute equaliser!

In January of that season I went to Griffin Park for an FA Cup 4th round tie against Brentford. I met up with Kieran Doran, not one of the original "Dublin Clarets" but nevertheless an Irish fan of Burnley, who just happens to be the most animated and excitable fan you could wish to meet. We were given tickets for the stand but we transferred to the terraces for the atmosphere (there were plenty of travelling Clarets). It is fair to say that we were battered by Brentford, but we still managed to win, 3-0. We had a good FA Cup run that season. I saw our tie against Fulham, who were using QPR's ground that season, and I also made the trip to Watford for the quarter final. Against Watford, Stan left Little and Blake on the substitutes bench until too late, and we limped out, 2-0.

We hung around the lower half of the table that season, eventually finishing 16th, not really being threatened by relegation after recovering from a poor start. That would soon change.

Tearful Farewell

The 2003-04 season was good in patches, but awful in even bigger patches. We started with three defeats, followed by three victories. I then saw my first game of the campaign, away at Norwich.
At the time, Norwich were planning a new stand, so the "away end" consisted of two rows of seats, spreading the whole length of one side. This arrangement hardly helped to generate any sort of atmosphere, all I remember is a

very sunny day, Burnley wearing the grey "VK" strip and getting introduced to Alastair Campbell by Allen Rycroft. We lost, 2-0.
Coincidentally, I met Alastair Campbell at the next away game, two weeks later. This was Wimbledon's first game at the National Hockey Stadium in Milton Keynes. A number of Clarets refused to attend the game, as it would encourage "franchise football" and I must admit I did give it plenty of thought. Campbell was doing a sponsored run somewhere and he managed to get a fiver off me for that!

Fast forward just over two weeks and I found myself watching a midweek game at Ipswich, sitting not too far from (you've guessed it) Alastair Campbell. At half-time we were 5-0 down but hardly any Burnley fans left early, indulging instead in a certain amount of "gallows humour". Ipswich took it easy after the break and we only lost 6-1. A few days later, I paid my first and only visit to the Boleyn Ground, the home of West Ham United. Unlike the capitulation at Ipswich, we battled hard for a creditable 2-2 draw.

My birthday in 2003 was spent at The Stadium Of Light as Burnley came from behind to snatch a 1-1 draw. I met Allen Rycroft in a Park And Ride location and we went by bus to the ground. Our scarves gave away who we were, but the Sunderland fans on the bus were really friendly, before and after the game.

We had our customary crisis over Christmas in 2003, losing four consecutive league games and finding ourselves in 21st place. The second half of the season was going to be a struggle.

At the end of 2003, I terminated my 33 year connection with Hotpoint, leaving as Export Director. I visited 46 different countries during my time with them and I had a stack of memories, which I have written about elsewhere. I started my own export consultancy business and I only made three overseas business trips thereafter. So, more time with my family – and more time with the Clarets!

I was able to catch more home games after the turn of the year, but our form was poor and we dropped too many home points. One of the away games I saw was the visit in late March to Bradford City, who were also struggling at the wrong end of the table. The second half saw one of the finest displays I have seen from a Burnley goalkeeper. With the score at 1-1, the home side threw everything at us, but Brian "Beast" Jensen produced a number of outstanding saves to stop us from going behind. We really were battered, but then Ian Moore headed a 90th minute winner. Talk about daylight robbery!

After the Bradford game, we proceeded to lose at home to Norwich and Watford, so we found ourselves on 24th April facing a desperate relegation shoot-out at Turf Moor against fellow-strugglers, Derby County. The tension could be felt in the ground well before kick-off and this built as the game progressed. Both sides were nervy and scared to make mistakes. Then Graham Branch cut in from the left wing and scored with a low shot into the far corner. The place erupted, as we saw an escape route for ourselves. We managed to hang on and created a little breathing space over our rivals – which was just as well as we lost our remaining two games.

Our penultimate game was at Rotherham. There was a fan there with a banner which stated "1972 was a wonderful year. Graham Branch was born". It was the only bright spot as we lost 3-0 and the board had made a significant announcement. They had decided to terminate the contract of Stan Ternent at the end of the season – in one week's time.

Stan's final match was against his boyhood favourites, Sunderland. It would have been lovely for him to have gone out with a victory but we concocted a 2-1 defeat. Even so, Stan received a memorable (and fully-deserved) ovation at the end of the game, from Burnley fans and also from those wonderful Sunderland fans.

Stan had done a magnificent job in turning the club around, restoring our self-respect and providing a platform upon which we could build. He was a no-nonsense, "hard as nails" character who you'd want alongside you if you encountered danger in a dark alley. But the emotional farewell from Burnley and Sunderland fans got to him and he left the pitch with tears streaming down his face.

In 2004 I formed my own consultancy and decided to become incorporated, as Exportential Limited. This necessitated my attending a company directors' briefing session at Companies House in Cardiff. I travelled to Cardiff the night before the session and I found out that Wales were playing Northern Ireland that night.

The match was a bad-tempered 2-2 draw, with Robbie Savage getting sent off. But it was my first visit to what was then called the Millennium Stadium – and I was very impressed. Somehow a brand new stadium had managed to retain the atmosphere of the old Arms Park. I have since attended a speedway Grand Prix at the stadium and the atmosphere was just as good.

Cotterill Building On Stan's Foundations

Burnley's new manager was Steve Cotterill, a positive appointment, who arrived as an ex striker but who tightened up our defence. In Stan's "Goals Galore" season, we conceded 89 goals but in Cotterill's first season we only conceded 39 goals – fewer than the champions, Sunderland. The problem was our "Goals For" column.

During the Steve Cotterill era, I was able to attend a lot more home games, without actually taking the plunge and investing in a season ticket. I occasionally used to buy the blocks of four tickets – you got four consecutive games in the same seat, which was a bit like a mini season ticket. As I no longer had to travel abroad, I was also able to get to more midweek away games (I remember Barnsley, Coventry, Ipswich and Luton among others).

Under Steve's management, we finished comfortably in mid-table in 2004-05 and again in 2005-06. The following season was a strange one – a good top half position leading up to Christmas, a truly awful run after Christmas but still only conceding 49 goals. Between 28th November and 31st March, we failed to win any of our 18 league games. If it hadn't have been for a late surge, winning five out of six games, we could have been in trouble.

I liked Steve Cotterill. He was good with the media, I liked his pitch-side behaviour and he certainly did a good job on our defence. Back in 2000 we wondered if Burnley could stay in the second tier having been promoted. Stan Ternent's foundation, followed by Steve Cotterill's consolidation meant that we were regularly in the top 30 teams in the country.

The 2007-08 season didn't start too badly, as we only lost one of our first eight matches. In mid-September I went to see us play at Sheffield Wednesday and I thought we played well to win 2-0. However, on 8th November, the board decided that a run of one win in ten games was in danger of becoming as disastrous as the previous season's 18 game run. So Steve Cotterill was sacked.

The new man was Owen Coyle, a former Bolton striker who had done well as the manager of St. Johnstone.

After Cotterill's sacking, we played six games without defeat, reaching 7th place in the league. But our form for the rest of the season was inconsistent and we finished in 13th place – well out of trouble but not promising a play-off spot either.

CHAPTER 16

WHY POSH CLARET?

"They're the second-best team in the world and there's no higher praise than that." (Kevin Keegan)

"I'd been ill and hardly trained for a week and I'd been out of the team for three weeks before that. So, I wasn't sharp and I got cramp before half-time as well. But I'm not one to make excuses." (Clinton Morrison)

From the mid 1980s, almost every club saw the introduction of football fanzines, some of which were provocative, challenging, satirical and downright funny. They were almost an extension of the irreverent university rag magazines.

I regularly used to buy fanzines, not just my own club's but also opposing teams' fanzines. I used to come across some genuinely funny articles but I also found that my own club's fanzines helped me, as a remote fan, to keep in touch with the club and its fans. You could watch news reports, read newspapers and hear radio interviews – but fanzines would tell it like it was, especially when it came to comments about rival clubs!

In the pre-Internet days, fanzines performed a valuable service – even if they did sometimes get perilously close to libel suits! Most of them used to invite articles and letters from fellow fans and I noticed that a number of Burnley fans used pen-names like "Clitheroe Claret", "Doncaster Claret" or "Norfolk Claret". I felt that "Peterborough Claret" was too long-winded, so I opted instead for "Posh Claret" – being a Clarets fan living near Peterborough and not being a Clarets fan who is smart and fashionable!

Fast forward to the introduction of online messageboards and discussion groups. These started to make the old fanzines somewhat redundant (although I still love a hard copy booklet to read) and became very popular, many surviving to this day. For the purpose of being recognised by other contributors and to enable yourself to "log in" to the messageboard, everyone needed to have a user name or password, or both. Again, I noticed that many of the Burnley fans used their location, followed by "Claret" – so it became "Bacup Claret", "Derby Claret", "Cumberland Claret" and so on. As with fanzines, I decided to use

"Posh Claret" as my online name (and of course it was easy to remember).

Moving well into the new millennium, social media platforms appeared and it soon became apparent to me that some platforms would suit my business needs and others would be more appropriate for non-business activities. I used LinkedIn very early for my business activities – and still do, mainly to promote the books I have written. I was never keen on Facebook, but I used Twitter a lot. Initially I used it just for business, using the handle @Exportential. But I soon saw how I could use Twitter to keep up to date with all things Burnley. In line with my fanzine and messageboard name, I decided to use @PoshClaret as my Twitter handle and I still use it today.

I have used Twitter to pick up official and rumoured club news, especially when we are approaching transfer deadlines. But I used to use it a lot to follow matches in progress, as a number of Twitter users were posting regular updates. When there was no other coverage, I was really grateful to other Twitter users for helping me to stay in touch.

I can't pretend to be a regular contributor as Posh Claret, although I have made a number of comments over the years. I am more of a "taker" of information – often laughing out loud at some of the stuff which is posted.

When the time came to give this book a title, it really did not take long, "Posh Claret" it had to be.

CHAPTER 17

OVERSEAS GAMES

"Real possession football this. And Zico's lost it." (John Helm)

"Djimi Traore had to adapt to the English game. And he did that by going out on loan to Lens last season." (Ian Rush)

I have explained how my work often took me away from the UK, often for several nights at a time. I got to know a number of overseas clubs by watching the local television in hotel rooms. But, occasionally, I got lucky and found myself in a location on a day when I could actually get along and watch a live match.

My first experience was in September 1987 when my Greek distributor took me along to watch his favoured team, **Aris Salonika**, playing against Larissa. The game was played in tremendous heat – and I was more concerned about surviving the sweltering heat than watching the game. The seller of bottled water made a fortune that day.
The standard of football was not bad, it became cooler in the second half and Aris lost to the team who became the eventual Greek champions that season.

My second match in Greece took me to Aris' fierce local rivals, **PAOK Salonika**. They were playing OFI from Crete. My main memory of the occasion is not the quality of the football but how intimidating the excitable crowd was. One of the linesmen was clearly scared stiff and proceeded to give some diabolical decisions in favour of the home side. Later, I discovered that a previous head coach at PAOK had been Les Shannon, the former Burnley player.

I had a very good customer in Spain, located at Mondragon in the Basque country. He liked early morning meetings on Mondays, which meant that I used to fly into Bilbao on Sunday evenings, probably arriving at about 7pm. On one occasion, I could only get a flight arriving at 3pm, so I checked in to my hotel much earlier than usual. Upon chatting in the hotel foyer, I discovered that the local team, **Athletic Bilbao**, were playing Valencia at 7pm, so I made my way to the stadium, used my pidgin Spanish to purchase a ticket, and found my seat. I don't look much like a Basque local and the two fans next to me soon discovered I was British. As Howard Kendall was the manager of Athletic Bilbao at the time, this made me instantly popular. The match was controlled by the visitors from Valencia, who won 4-1. The referee for the match was officiating for the last time before his retirement, so both teams lined up at the end and applauded as he left the pitch. Imagine such respect in England!

Towards the end of 1992, I flew into Madrid for a Monday morning meeting and I found myself in my hotel at about 3pm on the Sunday afternoon. A quick conversation with the hotel concierge and then I was in a taxi, bound for one of the most famous football grounds in the world, the Santiago Bernabéu Stadium, the home of **Real Madrid**. I made the mistake that several visiting spectators make by observing that it doesn't look all that big from the outside. That is because the playing surface is many feet lower than the ground outside, so when you walk in you actually go <u>down</u> to your seat, not up. It is a magnificent stadium, the atmosphere was electric, and not a little partisan! Real beat Celta Vigo with a single goal, less than ten minutes from the end.

The same thing happened to me in April 1993, I arrived in Madrid early on Sunday for a Monday meeting but this time I checked in advance and learned that Real Madrid were at home again. They played relegation-threatened Cadiz, who took an early lead before Real struck with three goals to win the game quite comfortably. I was disturbed by the attitude of the Real fans towards a black Cadiz winger but Real had a decent side and the occasion was otherwise very pleasant. I walked back to my hotel, to find that some of the other meeting delegates would have joined me had they known where I had gone. Regrettably, Cadiz were relegated at the end of the season.

During the 1990 World Cup tournament, a colleague and I found ourselves at the International Trade Fair in Malta. We made it clear to our hosts that we would like to see the **England v Cameroon** quarter final tie. It was worked out that there wouldn't be time for us to leave the Fair grounds and get back to our hotel in time to see the game. So, our distributor set up a large screen, plenty of seats and plenty of beer so we could watch the game on his exhibition stand, after the punters had left. We saw the game, and the extra time period, which ended up with England through to the semi-final. Then came the celebrations. When it came to football, half of Malta supported Italy and the other half supported England. On our way back to the hotel, we encountered numerous trucks and vans with very loud Union Jack wavers – and this lasted for most of the night.

Often, when I stayed in Dublin, I would use a hotel quite close to Lansdowne Road, the home of Irish rugby and also where the Ireland national football team played. On one occasion I opened my window and I could actually hear the crowd cheering. Subsequently, I picked up on the fact that my visit in April 1992 would coincide with the **Ireland v U.S.A.** international friendly match. I had no difficulty buying a ticket from a surprisingly reasonable ticket tout outside the ground and found my seat. Irish football was on fire at the time, with Jack Charlton in charge. I was aware of a problem that Irish visitors had been getting when applying for visas covering entry into the U.S.A. At the end of an entertaining match, which

Ireland won 4-1, the spectator next to me bellowed "now will ye give us our feckin' visas?" Great fun!

In June 1998, I found myself in Antwerp for a trade fair after having driven up from France. The Sales Director from my local distributor knew that I was a keen football fan and he invited me to attend a special showing at the City Hall of the **Belgium v Netherlands** World Cup group match. I accepted before realising that the "special showing" was for a load of Antwerp celebrities, officials and dignitaries. Apparently, the tickets had been quite expensive, as the price included a lavish meal and pre-match entertainment. We were all equipped with rattles, clackers and whistles, which we used with great gusto, maybe due to the excellent De Koninck beer which was being served. I was an honorary Belgian for the evening, shouting at the large screen along with the locals. The game itself was a nervy 0-0 stalemate, the highlight of which was Patrick Kluivert's red card.

I watched the **England v Argentina** game in the 1998 World Cup in a hotel foyer at Heathrow airport. There were about thirty local fans in there, plus two Argentinians, who left before the end.

In August 1998, I attended a trade fair at a remote place in Norway called Storefjell. The trade visitors arrived either for the first two days or for the second two days, which meant that the middle evening saw just the exhibitors and organisers present. We were treated to local food, served in a kind of very large wigwam. Afterwards nearly everyone gathered in front of a large screen to watch the **Norway v Romania** international friendly game. Despite my support as an honorary Norwegian, the game was a disappointing goalless draw.

After an early meal, my boss and I watched the 1999 **Manchester United v Bayern Munich** European Cup Final in a German beer garden in Düsseldorf. Neither of us had any love for United (he was a Halifax Town fan) and so we weren't terribly bothered that Bayern took an early lead. However, as the game progressed, the Germans in the beer garden turned it into a Germans versus English event and started to loudly mock us "losers". When United scored their two late goals to steal the match and win the trophy, that was the only time either of us had cheered for United. And I doubt if we ever will again!

I did try to see a rugby international in Paris, but without success. My colleague and I flew over on a Friday evening and the England rugby team were on the same flight as us. After a busy Saturday morning preparing a trade fair stand, we called it a day at lunchtime. We then made our way to Parc des Princes, to see if we could get tickets from spivs for the **France v England** international. To cut a long story short, we failed to find tickets at acceptable prices ("I am not paying that much just to watch England" said my colleague), so we spent a couple of hours walking around the Louvre instead.

Incidentally, my Welsh colleague would have supported France if we had got in, but I would have supported England. Just different types of Welshmen!

This doesn't count as an overseas game, but I did catch one Scottish match, a Scottish League Cup game between Dundee and St. Johnstone in August 1969. This was in the middle of a camping holiday with three mates. The visitors won 2-1, after their fans had tried to demolish a corrugated iron stand! We brave lads hot-footed it to safety.

CHAPTER 18

WEMBLEY (PROMOTION 2)

"I love Blackpool. We're very similar. We both look better in the dark." (Ian Holloway)

"If a Frenchman goes on about seagulls, trawlers and sardines, he's called a philosopher. I'd just be called a short Scottish bum talking crap." (Gordon Strachan)

When Owen Coyle assumed the manager's job at Burnley, he inherited some decent players – people like Brian Jensen, Michael Duff, Steven Caldwell, Wade Elliott, Chris McCann, Graham Alexander and Robbie Blake. His first half season went well enough, the Clarets finishing in a comfortable mid table position. One of the players Coyle added to the squad before the 2008-09 season was Chris Eagles, an exciting talent who was a former Manchester United youth player. Another was striker, Martin Paterson.

By this time, I was attending far more home games, taking advantage of the occasional blocks of four special offers. My working arrangements gave me more flexibility and I was able to incorporate more Clarets games into my diary. But I still hadn't taken the plunge and committed to a season ticket. During this period, if I struggled to get a ticket, Allen Rycroft would somehow help me out.

The first game of the 2008-09 season was miserable for Burnley and for me, personally. We were well beaten, 4-1, and I discovered after the game that I had lost my phone. I called Sheffield Wednesday FC, who confirmed that no phone had been handed in. By the time I had cancelled the phone, two overseas calls had already been made, which was not very pleasant.

League Cup Heroics

We only lost one game out of thirteen during the autumn, and we had climbed up to fourth in the league by early November. We were also putting together a decent run in the Football League Cup and we caused a big surprise when we beat Premier League Chelsea (on penalties) and Arsenal to qualify for the semi-final. From Boxing Day, we lost five consecutive league games and yet we were still in with a good chance of the play-offs as we prepared for the two-legged League Cup semi-final against Tottenham.

I bought my ticket for the second leg (at home) and I knew that it would only be the second time I had seen Burnley play in a semi-final in my life (the previous time was also in the League Cup, against Liverpool in 1983). The match was televised, we were awful, and Spurs won 4-1.

The second leg was written off by the press as a foregone conclusion, but it proved to be one of the bravest performances I have ever seen from a Burnley side. We went at Spurs from the outset and, just as they thought they had weathered the Burnley storm, Robbie Blake gave us a 1-0 lead, which we held until the break. The effort continued in the second half and Chris McCann added a second goal just over quarter of an hour from the end. Turf Moor erupted with two minutes to go, when local boy Jay Rodriguez scored a third Burnley goal. Incredibly we had given a good Premier League side three goals start and levelled on aggregate at 4-4.

The Football League Cup that year had a rule whereby, if the scores were level on aggregate, the side scoring the most away goals would prevail – but only after extra time. So, we played thirty minutes of extra time, we conceded two late goals and missed out on a Wembley final against Manchester United. But what a magnificent effort and what a piece of motivation from Owen Coyle.
I felt so proud of the team. The following day, I drove up to a trade fair in Newark. On the way home, I pulled into a lay-by, reflected on the events of the night before, and cried.

Push For The Play-Offs

Coyle had wound up his side to achieve miracles in the League Cup but he now had to pick them up after their disappointment and drive them towards the play-offs.

We continued our giant-killing in the FA Cup, by beating Premier League West Bromwich Albion and then came a cropper against Arsenal. But the league was our priority and a measure of the way in which Coyle kept the team fully focussed is the fact that we only lost two of our last 17 league games.

As the season moved towards "the business end", it was becoming very clear that we had a real chance of making the play-offs and the home crowds were on the increase. If we achieved promotion, then getting tickets could be a challenge. I therefore took up an offer to buy a part season ticket until the end of the season – and its renewal would guarantee me a seat for the following season, irrespective of which division we were in.

In mid-March we stuck 4 goals past Crystal Palace and 5 goals past Nottingham Forest, as we consolidated our place among the play-off positions. Our form had been good, but so had our rivals been picking up points, and we went into our final game, at home to Bristol City, knowing that a win was necessary but it would guarantee our place in the play-offs. We were excellent, Graham Alexander scored two more penalties, and we won 4-0. We could look forward to a two-legged play-off semi-final against Reading.

	Football League Championship : 2008-09					
		P	W	D	L	Pts
1.	Wolverhampton W.	46	27	9	10	90
2.	Birmingham City	46	23	14	9	83
3.	Sheffield United	46	22	14	10	80
4.	Reading	46	21	14	11	77
5.	Burnley	46	21	13	12	76
6.	Preston North End	46	21	11	14	74

Reading

Reading were a decent side, well managed by Steve Coppell, but they had been relegated from the Premier League the previous season and were keen to make an instant return. They would not be easy opponents.

The first leg at Turf Moor was a tense affair and Reading were well-deserved to be level, especially as they had the best player on the field, centre back Andre Bikey. But six minutes from time, Bikey threw a wobbly, conceded a penalty, got himself sent off and Burnley had a 1-0 lead to take into the second leg. Reading's best player would be suspended from the second leg, which helped our cause even further. Bikey would go on to join Burnley and was a popular player at the club.

As I mentioned earlier, my mate Allen Rycroft had queued for over 2 hours in the pouring rain, in order to get me a ticket for the second leg.

I had a business meeting in Derby on the morning of the match. When you want to drive from Peterborough to Reading, going via Derby is not the most logical route to take. Even so, I got there in good time, got parked easily enough, then met Alan Jackson and (former Clarets player) Rob Higgins for a natter before the game. The atmosphere amongst the travelling fans was electric – could we defend our lead and reach Wembley?

Reading were the better side in the first half, putting a lot of pressure on our defence and we were very relieved to go in at half-time with a 0-0 scoreline. But then, within 15 minutes of the re-start, the tie had been won. Firstly, Martin Paterson picked up the ball on the halfway line, ran straight for the penalty area and hit a magnificent shot inside the far post. That was the finest goal I have ever seen from a Burnley player – and what a time to get it! Just eight minutes later, Steven Thompson picked up a long clearance from Brian Jensen, allowed the ball to bounce and then lobbed it past the Reading keeper. The ball bounced down off the crossbar and then bounced up into the roof of the net.

With a three goal deficit to claw back, there was very little Reading could do but watch the visiting fans bouncing up and down, singing "Que Sera, Sera". Two memorable goals, an outstanding away day and now we were going to Wembley.

Sheffield United at Wembley

The other play-off semi-final had been a little closer than ours, but Sheffield United had only missed an automatic promotion place by three points. We knew that we would be in for a tough match but we still travelled with optimism.

I decided to go down by train and there seemed to be quite a lot of Blades fans on my train into King's Cross. I was surprised at how pessimistic they were, quoting Sheffield United's poor track record in play-off matches. When I arrived at the stadium, I met with Nigel Truswell, an old work colleague whose passion for Sheffield United matches my own for Burnley. Nigel had previously joined me as an honorary Claret at Peterborough, Stoke and Fulham. We both then met with Vincent Fean, whose ticket was for one of the more expensive seats, hence his suit and tie. Nigel had introduced me to Vincent (now Sir Vincent) in 2000, as they had been at University together. Nigel found that he knew two Burnley fans and thought that they should meet.

I found my seat, which was adjacent to those occupied by Allen Rycroft, Rob Higgins and Alan Jackson. The day was sunny, the atmosphere couldn't have been better, the two sets of fans were noisy and we just needed the right result. Early in the match, Wade Elliott scored with an excellent shot from outside the area. We had chances to extend our lead, but it remained 1-0 and the last fifteen minutes were tortuous. Allen Rycroft suggested that "of course we won't hang on. We wouldn't be Burnley if we got to the Premier League!" But he was wrong and when the final whistle blew, I just let out the loudest shriek I have ever mustered – all those bad experiences and frustrations in the lower divisions were immediately exorcised when that whistle blew. Apart from family matters, that final whistle was the highlight of my life. From the depths of near-oblivion at the Orient Game, we had gone all the way up to the Premier League. Little old Burnley had become "big time" again!

There were memorable scenes in the royal box and on the pitch when the trophy had been presented. My journey home was a joy, as fans of all sorts of other clubs congratulated me. What a wonderful day out! Thank you, Owen Coyle.

CHAPTER 19

SEASON TICKETS IN THE PREMIER LEAGUE

"Not to win is guttering." (Mark Noble)

"All that remains is for a few dots and commas to be crossed." (Mitchell Thomas)

Following my decision near the end of the previous season, I had a shiny new season ticket at the start of the 2009-10 season – our first season in the top division since 1976. I reckoned that if the coming season was going to be our only Premiership season, at least I would see all the home games, and a fair few away games too. The first home game was against the reigning champions, Manchester United. A superb Robbie Blake volley gave us an early lead and then, despite having to ride our luck at times, we held on for a famous victory. When you drive long distances to football matches, you will find yourself in motorway service stations, often with other clubs' fans. They ask who you have played and how you got on, so you can imagine my pleasure after that United victory in telling everyone I met how we had secured such a great result.

During that season I got to see our visits to Anfield, Old Trafford and the Emirates Stadium. Although the results weren't favourable, it was a great experience to see Burnley at such prestigious grounds, playing against some of the best players in the world.

Coyle – from Moses to Judas

Until mid-Autumn, we had a tendency to win our home games and lose our away games. We continued to perform badly away but we then started dropping points at home. As Christmas drew closer, we were starting to get a little too close to the relegation zone. And then it happened! Halfway through the season, Owen Coyle jumped ship and joined our relegation rivals, Bolton Wanderers. Plenty has been written about Coyle's departure, suffice it to say that the way the situation was handled by Coyle and Bolton Wanderers was less than dignified, with Coyle arguing that Bolton were "ten years ahead of Burnley". This was very sad, especially after the superb way he had led and inspired his team the previous campaign. But he had gone and we just had to move on without him.

Life Of Brian

The board responded by appointing our former full-back, Brian Laws, to the position of manager. Laws had a reputation for
1. working within a tight budget and
2. knowing the second tier very well

I am sure he was a very nice bloke, but I just felt that his appointment was tantamount to throwing in the towel and accepting our fate in the bottom three. It was not inspiring.

Our form after Laws' appointment was not good. The worst performance was a 6-1 defeat to Manchester City at home in early April (we had been 5-0 down at halftime). The 4-1 win the following week at Hull City (our only away victory) was very enjoyable, but the writing was on the wall by then and we slipped out of the Premier League one year after going up.

Premier League : 2009-10						
		P	W	D	L	Pts
17.	West Ham United	38	8	11	19	35
18.	Burnley	38	8	6	24	30
19.	Hull City	38	6	12	20	30
20.	Portsmouth	38	7	7	24	19

In the "bad old days" of Division Four, of course I would have snatched anyone's hand off for just one season in the Premier League, but when you have got that far, you want more. Steven Fletcher had been a good signing but I had been disappointed with Chris Eagles. I expected him to do well in the Premier League, and perhaps force his way into the England squad. But it didn't quite happen for him at that level. Looking forward to another Championship season under the uninspiring leadership of Brian Laws was not the greatest feeling – but I still hung on to my season ticket, though.

Burnley started the 2010-11 season reasonably well, although the away form remained poor. There was a spectacular 4-3 home victory over Preston with three late goals turning the match. We just couldn't buy an away victory and I attended a particularly lacklustre 1-0 defeat away at Coventry.

We were drifting in mid-table mediocrity, not helped by losing 3-2 at home to Leeds, after taking a 2-0 lead. Then, after a wretched home defeat by Scunthorpe United, Brian Laws was sacked. The board clearly felt that we needed a new direction. Before Laws' sacking, I witnessed our first away win of the season at Barnsley on Boxing Day. My daughter lived near Barnsley and I was able to sneak away from the festivities to catch a rare away win. In mid-January, Eddie Howe was confirmed as Laws' replacement.

Just Like Eddie

Howe was a bold and inspiring choice, having moved from playing to managing at Bournemouth. Initially the side did well under him but then a period of taking one point from six games condemned the Clarets to a finish of 8th, fully seven points short of the play-offs.

In Eddie's first full season, inconsistency was the key word. In September I witnessed a poor 2-1 defeat at my local club, Peterborough, although I did catch a belter of a goal from Keith Treacy. In November we suffered four consecutive defeats but bounced back with six wins in the next seven games. At that point we were 7th in the table, with play-off aspirations.

On 4th February 2012, I travelled by train for the Burnley v Peterborough match. As the game petered out into a 1-1 draw, the already-freezing conditions were accompanied by heavy snow. The uphill walk in slippery conditions was challenging, along with the thought that my train may be cancelled. Thankfully, my train was the last one to run before they dropped the guillotine and I found out through Twitter that not many cars got out of Burnley after 5.30pm that night. Coincidentally, sitting opposite me on the train was a bloke who I had last seen when I was umpiring a local Peterborough League cricket match in which he had played.

Further inconsistency in the new year saw us finish the 2011-12 season in a disappointing 13th position, although Jay Rodriguez's 15 goals and Charlie Austin's 16 goals had been highlights. I had been able to take my son-in-law to catch our 2-1 win at Doncaster late in the season.

At the start of the 2012-13 season, I felt reasonably confident, as we had a number of younger players coming through and Eddie Howe seemed likely to be there for some time to come. Wrong!

Again, we started the season inconsistently, losing our second, third and fourth matches but then battering Peterborough 5-2 (what a pleasant journey home that was). After ten games, we were sitting unimpressively in 16th place. And then Eddie resigned, citing family reasons.

Eddie Howe was popular with the fans, he came across well on the television and conducted his departure with dignity. We wished him well.

The season was notable because Charlie Austin scored 25 league goals but it was also notable because it saw the introduction of the man who would give Burnley fans some of our finest days ever. On 30th October 2012, Sean Dyche was appointed manager of Burnley.

CHAPTER 20

LINCOLN CITY

"For those of you watching in black and white, Spurs are in the all-yellow strip." (John Motson)

"I was really surprised when the F.A. knocked on my doorbell." (Michael Owen)

My first visit to Sincil Bank, the home of Lincoln City, was during our promotion push in 1982. Trevor Steven rescued a late point in a game we deserved to lose. I felt a little guilty having stolen a point, but the Imps would get their own back on me, in spades!

My wife and I started up a business networking club in Lincoln in September 2009. We regularly attracted over 50 business people to our fortnightly meetings and we developed a reputation for being good connectors of people. Lincoln City FC obviously made money from gate receipts and player sales but, like all other football clubs, they had a string of other revenue-earning activities to sell. So, I invited them to join our club and hopefully meet business people who were potential match sponsors, advertisers, executive box hirers and shirt sponsors. They agreed to join, on the understanding that we had a "cash neutral" arrangement. This meant that I spent with them whatever they spent with me.

My budget was never going to extend to shirt sponsorship or large-scale advertising, but there were a number of ways in which I could support the club, who were members of our business club of course. The most obvious way was to hire an executive box for a game, which proved to be very cost-effective. As box hirers, we got ten match tickets, free programmes, food and non-alcoholic drinks. There was a TV in each box and we received three or four parking spots at the ground. I used to invite five club members and four guests (who were potential members of course), meeting them for a beer in the club lounge before being taken to our box. To add further interest, I organised a sweep for the time of the first goal. Everyone enjoyed themselves and we got a good view of the match from our vantage point.

The first match I chose for our executive box was before Lincoln's relegation from the Football League. It was in March 2011 and the opponents were Rotherham United. Lincoln were appalling and got thumped 6-0. They didn't win a game before the end of the season and were relegated in 23rd position.

Over the next few seasons, Lincoln City had a dire time in the National League, sometimes flirting with relegation and never really threatening the play-offs. I continued to hire executive boxes, covering the matches against Fleetwood (lost 3-1 in October 2011), Southport (won 2-0 in January 2012), Cambridge United (lost 1-0 in April 2012), Nuneaton (won 2-1 in September 2012) and Luton Town (lost 2-1 in October 2012). My relationship with the club was further enhanced when I used their facilities (executive boxes and sponsors lounges) for training courses, seminars and presentations. Whenever I was in Lincoln with a couple of hours to spare between meetings, I used their various rooms, all of which were equipped with wifi and coffee. I had lots of friends in the club, but they were fully aware that my first footballing love was with Burnley.

In the summer of 2016, the fortunes of the Imps took an upward turn when Danny Cowley was appointed as manager (his brother Nicky was his assistant). The club stormed up to the top of the National League table and put together a very impressive FA Cup run, beating Ipswich and Brighton on their way to the 5th round. During one of our business club meetings, word got round that the cup draw had paired Burnley and Lincoln together, to be played at Turf Moor on 18th February 2017. Of course, I had no need to worry – Burnley were an established Premier League club and Lincoln were only playing in the National League, four divisions below us.

All my contacts in Lincoln teased me during the two weeks leading up to the game. I remembered Burnley losing to non-league Wimbledon back in 1975, although I hadn't attended the game. Surely, we would not slip up against Lincoln?

I travelled up to Burnley by train, being joined by loads of Lincoln fans at Newark, and even more of them from Doncaster. They were very boisterous and confident – but I looked forward to seeing them somewhat quieter on the return journey.

Burnley had achieved a lot of success by playing a pressing game against Premier League opponents, never letting them settle, and then catching them out from set pieces. That is exactly what Lincoln did to us and we got very impatient until Joey Barton got wound up and lost his temper. In the last seconds of the game, Lincoln scored the only goal from a corner – and we were out.

My journey home was thoroughly miserable, as were the next few weeks as I encountered Lincoln fans everywhere I went.

As well as getting promoted back into the Football League that season, Lincoln City did well from their cup run and picked up some much-needed cash. Many months after the cup game I attended a business presentation at Lincoln's new training facilities. As the group of about 50 were being shown around, our host said "a big thank you to Mike Stokes and everyone at Burnley – without whom, this would not have been possible".

I wish the Imps every success but I still squirm when I think back to that awful cup tie.

CHAPTER 21

ANTI-FOOTBALL

"I definitely want Brooklyn to be christened, but I don't know what religion yet." (David Beckham)

"I can see the carrot at the end of the tunnel." (Stuart Pearce)

I have had a season ticket at Turf Moor since 2009. My attendance at home matches had steadily increased, partly because my daughters had grown up, partly because my work no longer required me to go on frequent overseas trips and partly because Stan Ternent had got us out of the third tier. The Championship is an excellent league with some decent clubs playing at decent grounds.

When attending 3pm home matches, I carefully place a couple of Burnley scarves on the back parcel shelf and load up my grub for the day (my better half packs me up with enough food for lunch and for the evening journey home). I select an appropriate playlist on my phone and then push back off the drive at about 9am. Every journey to Turf Moor is special. As a remote fan, I don't visit the town of Burnley regularly. I didn't get to Burnley until I was 16 and my trips after then were very few and far between. It was always an enormous thrill to see the ground – and it still is!

I usually drive up the A1, joining the M62 near Pontefract. The heaviest traffic is usually around Leeds, as I head towards the Hartshead Moor service area. This is where I invariably encounter a variety of travelling football fans – sometimes Burnley fans but usually fans crossing the Pennines on their way to Liverpool, Manchester and the Lancashire clubs. When I hear of major roadworks I sometimes use the M18 and M1, taking me past Sheffield but still ending up at Hartshead Moor.

I don't use the M66 and M65, because that route brings me into Burnley at the wrong end for Turf Moor. So, after my pit stop, I have two choices – either come in through Sowerby Bridge, Hebden Bridge and Todmorden or leave the M62 later and come via Milnrow, Littleborough and Todmorden. Travelling through the Pennines or travelling over the Pennines can give me some spectacular scenery and there are few more picturesque views on a fine sunny day. Except that I don't see many sunny days! I usually encounter low cloud, dense walls of spray and loads of treacherous surface water. Nevertheless, I generally get parked after my 170 mile journey in Lebanon Street or Olympia Street before 1pm, devour my lunch while sitting in the car and then make my way to the Club Shop. The next stage in the fortnightly ritual is to join Alan, Roger, Andy, Stephen and Sandra in the Burnley Miners Social Club. We used to use the Burnley FC Foundation Lounge, and then the 110 Club – both of which are no longer available to us. We leave the Miners before 2.30pm, walk the short distance to the ground and meet Allen Rycroft for a natter before taking our seats.

My return journey also involves a food and loo stop at Hartshead Moor, this time coming across football fans on their way home after their respective matches. If we have lost, I am almost guaranteed to meet some opposing fans at the service station. The journey home can be really miserable after a defeat, especially when a radio pundit explains how bad we have been. With any luck, I arrive home just before 9pm.

So, when Burnley have home matches starting at 3pm, my schedule is well worked out and is pretty comfortable. My worst journey to Turf Moor took over six hours and resulted in my getting sat in my seat 20 minutes after kick-off. Sometimes bad traffic causes me to forego the Miners visit but generally I am in good time.

Evening matches are quite different. For a 7.45pm kick-off, I leave home at 1.45pm and follow a similar routine, although the early rush hour traffic around Leeds can be a pain. The return journey is an absolute lottery. Any regular motorway users will know that most overnight roadworks start at 8pm, so my journey home can be severely disrupted by road closures and diversions. One night the

M62 and the M1 were both closed and I found myself driving through the middle of Barnsley after midnight. Sometimes, the authorities will tease me by suddenly introducing a diversion late in my journey, say at Grantham or Stamford. I have often arrived home after 2am, which is all you need when you have just endured a home defeat. Travelling to evening games can be quite exhausting.

In 2011, to give me a change from all the driving, I decided to start using the train for some matches. I live only 9 miles from Peterborough station, which I can reach by bus or car, and trains are very frequent. The journey to Burnley is easy – Peterborough to Leeds and then Leeds to Burnley Manchester Road – and booking in advance with a Senior Railcard means the fares are not unreasonable. Travelling on the train means that I meet lots of other fans and over the years I have had some excellent conversations with fans of Brighton, Fulham, Luton, Charlton and Leeds. I was surrounded by a group of Crystal Palace fans on the train from Leeds once. I chatted to the guy who appeared to be the lead character for some time and then he cleared off to find a loo. His mate told me "blimey you are highly honoured, he normally falls out and gets aggressive with opposing fans." I also befriended a group of Southampton fans and as we got off the train one of them asked me if I knew any bars which were safe for visiting fans. I was able to show them the turning for Burnley Cricket Club, which always welcomes opposing supporters.

I always book early trains, so that I am down at the ground in good time. Coming home is not so easy, as the last train back from Leeds to Peterborough leaves at about 8.15pm. If my first train from Burnley is delayed I start worrying about making my connection. The worst journey I had was when my first train was cancelled so a replacement bus service was provided between Burnley and Leeds. I made my connection with less than 5 minutes to spare! The alternative would have been a hotel for the night in Leeds. Arriving by train is easy because I have a long downhill walk from the station to the town. But, of course, the reverse is true for the return journey. That damn hill seems to get steeper every time I huff and puff my way up it! But the biggest problem with using the train is not weather or slightly late arrivals, it is regular industrial action. To get a decent fare I need to book early and then, when industrial action is taken, I have to cancel my tickets. In recent years, I have become sick and tired of this, so I have stopped using the train. As I get older, I will find the 340 mile round trip to be more of a challenge, so I just hope that the railways industrial action is a thing of the past by then.

Introduction of Dyche

I must confess that I didn't know too much about Sean Dyche when he was named as Burnley's new manager. I remember him as an inspiring captain of Chesterfield, leading them to a memorable FA Cup semi-final against Middlesbrough in 1997. He played for a few other clubs and there is a clip on YouTube of him putting in a wild tackle while playing for Northampton Town – it resulted in a red card for the innocent-looking Dyche. After retiring, he became a manager and was fired from Watford for having committed the crime of not being Italian! The owners of Watford, the Pozzo family, clearly wanted Gianfranco Zola in charge and Dyche was unfairly dumped. He seemed to have done a reasonable job at

Watford and his dismissal was harsh. Boy, did we benefit from that decision!

Sean Dyche joined us at the end of October 2012 with the Clarets sitting in 14th position in the Championship. His first part-season was steady enough as we won 11 games and lost 11 games between his appointment and the end of the season. After three consecutive wins in January, we jumped up to 7th place, but then we only collected one win in twelve games, so by the season's end we had dropped to 11th. A satisfactory start.

Promotion and Runners Up

Our start to the 2013-14 season was spectacular, losing only one of our first 16 games. We were top of the Championship table, with Sam Vokes and Danny Ings building a prolific scoring partnership. Sean Dyche was increasingly impressive, handling the media with aplomb and giving the fans much optimism. Despite the odd flicker, we had been pretty average since losing our Premier League status in 2010 but we were getting more and more confident that Dyche was the man to take us back to the promised land.

In September 2013, I attended my first game at Elland Road, home of the notorious "Dirty Leeds". We played really well and despite Leeds throwing everything at us in the second half, we hung on for a deserved 2-1 victory. On Boxing Day, we lost to Middlesbrough but we only lost two more games between then and the end of the season. One of the games we lost was at home to Leicester City, the eventual champions and the only side better than us. In April, I went with my son-in-law to see a hard-fought 1-0 victory at Barnsley, with Ashley Barnes getting the winner.

Promotion was confirmed in the home game against Wigan Athletic, ironically one of the few home games I missed that season. It was my younger daughter's birthday and we had a nice family day together, occasionally catching Sky Sports to monitor our progress. I managed to attend the final home game, at which I bought a new tee shirt, printed "We Are Premier League".

In his first full season, Dyche had got us up to the Premier League, an outstanding achievement.

Football League Championship : 2013-14						
		P	W	D	L	Pts
1.	Leicester City	46	31	9	6	102
2.	Burnley	46	26	15	5	93
3.	Derby County	46	25	10	11	85
4.	Queen's Park Rangers	46	23	11	12	80

And Again …. What Goes Up ….

Having got us promoted to the Premier League, Dyche now faced the same dilemma as Owen Coyle – could he keep us there?

The season immediately after getting promoted to the Premier League is always tough and it is imperative to get off to a good start – which we didn't! After ten games, we found ourselves rock bottom and we did not secure our first victory until 9th November at home to Hull. Once again, my attitude was that these top-tier seasons re so precious that I will try and see as many as possible. The only home game I missed was the Boxing Day defeat to Liverpool. We went on a winless run after the New Year and it wasn't broken until a memorable victory at home to Manchester City, when George Boyd scored the only goal.

After the City game, we went six games without scoring (losing four consecutive games 1-0) and, despite being unbeaten in our final three games, we finished 19th and were relegated. We did the double over Hull City, who were relegated with us. Dean Marney's injury was a big blow, as he had been the heartbeat of the side. But the biggest problem was a shortage of goals, only Danny Ings scored more than ten. Our biggest defeat had not been against one of the "giants" but at West Bromwich Albion, where we lost 4-0. We only won two away games all season, and I caught one of them, the 1-0 win at Hull.

It looked for a long time that newly-promoted Leicester City would accompany us in relegation, but they put together a fantastic sequence of results, winning seven and drawing one of their last nine games. This sequence was continued the following season when they actually won the title.

Premier League : 2014-15						
		P	W	D	L	Pts
17.	Aston Villa	38	10	8	20	38
18.	Hull City	38	8	11	19	35
19.	Burnley	38	7	12	19	33
20.	Queen's Park Rangers	38	8	6	24	30

When teams get relegated, the manager usually gets fired, either as a panic measure with about six games to go, or as soon as relegation is confirmed. But the board at Burnley made the decision at the end of the season to stick with Sean Dyche and challenge him to get us back at the first attempt. It would prove to be an inspired decision.

Promotion and Champions

We started our promotion challenge early, hitting 3rd place by mid-September and remaining in the top 5 by Christmas. Goalkeeper Tom Heaton was turning in some outstanding performances, aided by the solid centre-back pairing of Michael Keane and Ben Mee. The experienced Joey Barton had an excellent time as a midfield general, demonstrating maturity and restraint. Up front we were scoring goals for fun, with Sam Vokes and André Gray proving difficult to contain. Scott Arfield had scored the only goal in a televised 1-0 victory at Ewood Park and will be remembered forever because of that.

On Boxing Day, we lost 3-0 at Hull City but we didn't lose another game all season. There were some memorable victories (4-0 over Bristol City, 5-0 over MK Dons and 4-1 over Derby County come to mind) but perhaps the most dramatic fixtures were the 2-2 draw at Brighton and the home 1-1 draw with Middlesbrough. Both games against our nearest rivals were saved by Michael Keane equalisers in added time and the results were typical of the attitude and spirit which had been instilled by Dyche. Promotion was confirmed when we beat Queens Park Rangers on 2nd May. To be crowned Champions, we needed a result from our last game, away at Charlton Athletic.

I had long admired Charlton, from the days when their supporters were dragged around London for ages using other clubs' grounds. But the fans helped to rebuild The

Valley so that they could return. As I hadn't been to The Valley before, I decided to attend the last game of the season – and it proved to be one of my most enjoyable away trips. The weather was glorious all day, which helped to make the train journey to King's Cross very pleasant. I tubed across to London Bridge station, where there was already a large gathering of Burnley fans. Amongst them, director Clive Holt was in good spirits. I had arranged to meet Vincent Fean for a catch-up before the game and it was good to have a coffee with him, not far from the stadium. And then I made my way to the ground, where I met up with my old friend from North Wales, Les Williams. This was the first time Les and I had met since Deepdale in 1973, so it was good to be introduced to his daughter over a couple of beers. Burnley ran out very comfortable winners, 3-0, and so were crowned champions.

During the match the Charlton fans staged an amusing sideshow when they ran along the back of the stand with a really long banner, suggesting that their owners were liars and cheats! They started chanting for the board to be removed, and the Burnley fans joined in with the chanting.

After the game there was mutual applause between the two sets of fans and the good humour continued on the journey back to London Bridge. Whilst walking down the platform, the tannoy announcer welcomed Burnley fans to the station and congratulated us on winning the title. Nice weather, nice people and nice result – if only all away games could be like that!

The directors' decision to stick with Dyche was absolutely the right one. He just needed now to show what he had learned from the year before and hopefully keep us in the Premier League.

Football League Championship : 2015-16					
		P	W	D	L	Pts
1.	Burnley	46	26	15	5	93
2.	Middlesbrough	46	26	11	9	89
3.	Brighton & Hove Albion	46	24	17	5	89
4.	Hull City	46	24	11	11	83

After the season finished, the 2016 Euros were upon us. The performance by the Welsh team was tremendous and they put in one of the best performances I have seen from a British team in a major competition in beating (2nd in the world) Belgium 3-1. The Welsh third goal was a wonderful header from the edge of the box by Burnley's own Sam Vokes and I remember Alan Shearer saying "that is a very good centre forward's goal".

During the summer after winning promotion, Dyche made four really useful signings. He brought in Nick Pope and Johann Berg Gudmundsson from Charlton, Jeff Hendrick from Derby and Steven Defour from Anderlecht. They would all make a big contribution over the years and they were very popular with the fans.

Consolidation

We opened up the 2016-17 season with a disappointing 1-0 home defeat against Swansea City but we followed that up with a sensational 2-0 victory over mighty Liverpool. I think we created a new Premier League record for winning a game with the smallest percentage possession figure. The following week, I went to see us play at Chelsea, my first visit to Stamford Bridge. My younger daughter was living in London at the time and she accompanied me to the game. We just couldn't handle Hazard and Willian, in fact Chelsea looked like scoring every time they attacked. We were somewhat flattered by the 3-0 result, it could have been worse.

We were inconsistent throughout the season, but we had to remember that we were fresh up from the Championship and we saw over and over again that the Premier League is so unforgiving. Every time we lost possession we seemed to get ruthlessly punished. But we weren't doing that badly. Very late winners against Everton and Crystal Palace took the roof off Turf Moor, then two wins in late December lifted us up to 11th place.

We beat the reigning champions, Leicester at the end of January but then we didn't win again until April. This period included that embarrassing FA Cup defeat at home to non-league Lincoln.

A home victory over Stoke and a point at the Riverside against Midlesbrough were useful but then, when we most needed it, we won away at Crystal Palace, to give us some breathing space. We only won a single point from our last three games, but we had already done enough and we finished in 16th place – safe from the drop.

Sean Dyche had built a talented side of fighters, players who did not know when they were beaten. We pressed opposing teams, never gave them time or space. And we were dangerous at set pieces. Dyche said "we are not going to succeed by out-passing the likes of Chelsea". We survived by playing our own style (perhaps too "long ball" for the purists) and it was very effective.

Dyche's team had achieved something we had not done since 1975 – we had survived a season in the top division without getting relegated.

Qualification for Europe

The 2017-18 season started off sensationally. Our first game was a really tough one – away at the reigning champions, Chelsea. I sat at home watching Sky Sports' Jeff Stelling update the nation with scores as they happened. After 24 minutes, Jeff reported that there had been a goal scored at Stamford Bridge – surprisingly by the away side! A quarter of an hour went by and he reported that Burnley had doubled their lead. Then, just before half-time, Sam Vokes made it 3-0. Burnley were leading the champions by three clear goals! In the second half, Chelsea turned on the style and clawed the game back to 3-2, which is how it stayed. What a start!
After a disappointing 1-0 home defeat to West Bromwich Albion, our next fixture was an away game at Tottenham Hotspur, who were playing their home games at Wembley that year. I was accompanied by my younger daughter and her Spurs-supporting boyfriend. He agreed to sit in the Burnley end and promised not to cheer if Harry Kane and his mates scored. Early in the second half, Spurs took the lead and looked like scoring more thereafter but, in front of nearly 68,000 people, our new signing, Chris Wood, equalised in added time. What a result!

That trip to Wembley was the last away match I attended. For some years I was troubled by an arthritic knee and I had a knee replacement operation in September 2017. Whilst the knee is far more comfortable than it used to be, if I take it for granted, it complains and lets me know about it. Which means that I just cannot stand up for two hours at football matches (nor at rock concerts).
Sitting in the Bob Lord stand at Turf Moor presents no problems because the people in that stand only stand up to greet the teams or to celebrate a goal. But, whenever you

attend a match as an away fan, you can't sit down because everyone else stands up, all through the game. Stewards don't bother to make the other fans sit down so there is nothing which can be done.

I will make an exception if we get to Wembley, but it looks unlikely I will see any more away games now. Following the Spurs game, we went a further five games without defeat. By the middle of October, we were in 7th position. Then, after an expected defeat at Manchester City, we won three games in succession. Two more victories from four games brought us to a midweek home fixture with Stoke City on 12th December 2017. I drove over 300 miles with constant rain in both directions, arriving home at 2pm. But I couldn't have been happier. Ashley Barnes scored the only goal of the game in the 89th minute. This victory took us up to 4th place in the Premier League, our highest league position since 1975.

There was even a chance we could qualify for Europe!

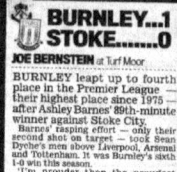

Premier League : 12th December 2017						
		P	W	D	L	Pts
1.	Manchester City	16	15	1	0	46
2.	Manchester United	16	11	2	3	35
3.	Chelsea	17	11	2	4	35
4.	Burnley	17	9	4	4	31
5.	Liverpool	16	8	6	2	30
6.	Arsenal	17	9	2	5	29
7.	Tottenham Hotspur	17	8	4	4	28

After the Stoke victory, we then went eleven games without a win. But this sequence included a very creditable draw at Old Trafford, where fans' favourite, Steven Defour, scored with an outstanding free kick. The Belgian, Defour, was hardly ever fully-fit during his time at Burnley but he was highly-regarded by the fans – one of our most talented players.

The barren sequence was ended by a run of five consecutive victories (and 15 more points) as we consolidated in 7th place. The second of these victories was at West Ham – a 3-0 away win which ended with the home fans throwing things on the pitch, at their own players, not at ours! Seventh was a position which we kept until the end of the season, five points clear of Everton in 8th.

This final league position resulted in Burnley qualifying for the Europa League. Our last European involvement had been when we reached the quarter final of the old Fairs Cup in the 1966/67 season. I don't know who won the "Manager of the Year" award in 2018 – presumably someone in charge of a group of precocious millionaires. But we all knew who should have received the award.

Sean Dyche's achievement in getting Burnley from mid-table in the Championship to European qualification was nothing short of remarkable. When comparing him to other Burnley managers, only Harry Potts stands above him – and don't let us forget that Harry's players were subjected to the maximum wage restrictions and couldn't therefore be enticed away.

From Başakşehir to Burton

Because of our European activity, the 2018-19 season started for Burnley on 26th July, with an away tie in the Europa League against Aberdeen. We drew the first leg and won the second game, to progress on aggregate. I remember taking my seat before the second leg, simply marvelling at the prospect of the Clarets playing European football again.

Our second tie was against the Turkish team, Başakşehir Istanbul and we went through by scoring the only goal of the tie in extra time of the home leg. Our European luck ran out against Greek team, Olympiakos of Athens. We lost the first leg 3-1 but could only manage a 1-1 draw in the home leg. So, the little adventure was over but at least I had seen the three home legs.

One of our early fixtures saw us lose a League Cup tie at Burton Albion, which brought us down to earth after our European involvement. So from Başakşehir to Burton within a couple of weeks!

Unfortunately, our European distractions had an adverse effect upon our domestic performances. We drew one and lost four of our first five games and then, after victories over Bournemouth and Cardiff, we failed to win any of our next eight games. After the home defeat to Liverpool on 8th December we were 19th out of twenty. Once again, I missed the Boxing Day fixture, which was just as well as we lost 5-1 to Everton.

We picked things up after the Christmas period, impressively stringing together five wins and three draws in our next eight matches. In the remaining games, we managed to gather enough points to get clear of the relegation zone and we finished in a fairly respectable 15th. It was a tough season but we had shown admirable resilience.

In April 2019, Burnley gained a creditable 2-2 draw at Stamford Bridge. We were never going to get anything out of the game by trying to match the way that Chelsea played, so we did what Burnley did best – we pressed on Chelsea, we gave them no time, we gave them no space, and we put ourselves about, especially Ashley Barnes, who was being marked by David Luiz. Chelsea were annoyed that Burnley hadn't just rolled over and given them the points. During the post-match interviews, David Luiz said that Burnley had played some sort of "anti football". The fans picked up on this and often sarcastically chanted "anti football" when we were stroking it about and unpicking opponents' defences.

Top Half Again

The 2019-20 season would ultimately end in a very strange way, due to substantial external influences, but it started reasonably enough for Burnley. Our autumn form was promising and, after beating Watford in late November, we had climbed up to 6th place in the table. We then proceeded to lose seven games out of nine, which ensured that the best we could expect was a mid-table position. An unbeaten 7-match sequence ensured that we were in a comfortable spot by late February.

On 7th March 2020 we drew with Tottenham – but then we didn't play another match for three months. Large gatherings of people were forbidden during the Covid pandemic, so all football was temporarily suspended. The Premier League re-started on 22nd June, no fans allowed though, with a 5-0 defeat at Manchester City. In order to get the 2019-20 season finished, spectator-free matches were crammed into a tight schedule, during which Burnley did well. After the City defeat, we only lost one more game – ironically it was the last game of the season against Brighton and we would have finished in 8th place (thus qualifying for the Europa League) if we had won. Instead we finished tenth, a highlight being the 14 goals scored by Chris Wood.

Close Shave

Burnley did not start the 2020-21 season well. After six games, we had picked up only one point, and we were bottom of the league. Our first victory was not achieved until 23rd November, followed the next week by our customary 5-0 defeat at Manchester City. An unlikely away win at Arsenal, together with wins over Wolves and Sheffield United, gave us hope going into the turn of the year.

On 21st January we went to Anfield, where Liverpool had not lost for 68 matches. Incredibly, we pulled off a 1-0 away victory, thanks to an Ashley Barnes penalty. Our form thereafter was inconsistent, but always just about keeping our heads above water. An impressive 4-0 victory at Wolves included a first half hat-trick by Chris Wood. And then we won 2-0 at Fulham to pretty much make ourselves safe. We lost our last three games, to finish in 17th place – only one place above relegated Fulham, although 11 points clear of them. It had been a tough season, but with one or two notable highlights. Once again, Sean Dyche had kept Burnley in the Premier League – but how much longer could he keep doing that?

Relegation and the Sack

Our poor end to the season continued into the 2021-22 season, although the signing of Maxwel Cornet, just before the transfer window closed, gave us a reason for optimism.

Our first victory did not come until 30th October – a Cornet-inspired 3-1 win over Brentford. I left home at 8.45am that day, experienced two substantial holdups due to motorway accidents, and it took me six and a half hours to reach Burnley. I took my seat at 3.20pm, by which time the Clarets were already ahead. It was a strange feeling outside of a packed stadium and I could hear the chant "Ole, Ole, Ole, Ole, Cornet, Cornet" so I knew who had scored our first goal.

A month after the Brentford game, I turned up to watch the home game with Tottenham Hotspur. The conditions had got increasingly more wintery as I got further north but I joined my mates in the Foundation Lounge to enjoy some pre-match chat. As we looked out of the window over the pitch we could see it snowing quite heavily. When the ground staff cleared the snow from the marked lines, the snow was so heavy that within a couple of minutes the lines were hidden again. The referee had no choice but to postpone the game, less than an hour before kick-off. Because the postponement had been so late, all the fans were already in Burnley, so I had a terrible job getting out of the place. After an hour, I had travelled about two miles – and the weather was still deteriorating. Eventually I reached the M62, which came to a standstill after less than ten miles due to an accident. It took me ages to get home – and, of course, we had not seen a game.

By the time we had reached mid-February, we had only won one game, we were well-entrenched in the relegation zone and Newcastle had taken our best striker, Chris Wood. Wood's replacement was Dutchman Wout Weghorst, who was far from impressive, to say the least. We then took seven points out of nine – including a 1-0 win in the re-arranged match against Spurs.

We followed that with just one win in six games, the last of which was a particularly inept performance, losing 2-0 at fellow strugglers, Norwich. It was the final straw, and the board did something which had been unthinkable a couple of years before, they sacked Sean Dyche.

Dyche had been the best managerial appointment in my time as a Burnley fan. I loved the spirit and camaraderie which he brought to the team. He also developed a number of players from "good" to "international" class (Heaton, Pope, Keane, Tarkowski) and he handled Joey Barton better than any of Joey's previous managers. We had enjoyed many good days under Dyche and we owed him a lot.

But I could understand why the board felt that they just had to be seen to be doing something, rather than "fiddling while Rome burns". They placed one of our coaches, Mike Jackson, as our caretaker manager until the end of the season – and it very nearly worked!

Jackson's first game was a good 1-1 draw at West Ham, then he followed this up with three consecutive victories, and nine points towards safety. With four games to go, Jackson had given us a real chance of survival. The bottom two clubs, Watford and Norwich, were goners but the third relegation spot was between Burnley, Leeds and

Everton. But we only took one point from those four games, including a final day home defeat to Newcastle. If we had won that last game, we would have stayed up, just ahead of Leeds on goal difference.

At the end of a thoroughly miserable season, we were back in the Championship, Sean Dyche had left the club and a new era was about to begin.

	Premier League : 2021-22					
		P	W	D	L	Pts
17.	Leeds United	38	9	11	18	38
18.	Burnley	38	7	14	17	35
19.	Watford	38	6	5	27	23
20.	Norwich City	38	5	7	26	22

CHAPTER 22

KOMPANY

"I don't have any tattoos, but that's mainly because none of my limbs are wide enough to support a visible image." (Peter Crouch)

"I always used to put my right boot on first, and then obviously my right sock." (Barry Venison)

Following our relegation, we lost a number of top performers – Nick Pope, James Tarkowski, Ben Mee, Nathan Collins, Dwight McNeil, Maxwel Cornet. It was obvious that the new manager would have to recruit quickly and, hopefully, effectively.

As soon as the season ended, speculation was rife on the message boards and on Twitter about who our new boss would be. Would the board go for a "name" or would they go for a lower division "safe pair of hands"?

I don't think any of us guessed correctly, so when Vincent Kompany was announced, it is fair to say that it was a surprise. I was not unhappy with the appointment. He had been one of the best defenders in the world, he had been an outstanding leader and he had cut his teeth as a coach with Anderlecht. It was an inspired choice and suggested that our board were absolutely intent on a speedy return to the Premier League.

Between his appointment as manager and the start of the new Championship season, Kompany was extremely busy in the transfer market, with a mixture of permanent transfers and season-long loan deals. He was readily available to the Press and explained that he would be implementing a passing game, playing out from the back. No more "long ball" stuff then!

An "OK" Start

Our first Championship match for over six years was a Friday night televised fixture at Huddersfield Town. It was obvious from the start that we would be keeping the ball down, maintaining possession for long periods and using our goalkeeper as a sweeping defender. For twenty

minutes it was tidy and encouraging. Then we scored through attacking full back, Ian Maatsen, one of our season-long loan players. We held on to our 1-0 lead and produced a very efficient away win. The first home game saw us draw with Luton Town and we witnessed how our new "playing from the back" style might cause us a few problems. The next game was a disappointing 1-0 defeat at Watford, which we followed with two home draws.
Our sixth match of the season was away at Wigan Athletic and we showed how all the changes in personnel were starting to work, with a 5-1 victory. On 25th October we beat Norwich and reached first place in the league – a position which we held for the rest of the season.

Our closest rivals in the league were Sheffield United and we received an almighty thrashing from them in November. They beat us 5-2 and exposed a very fragile weakness we had for crosses, especially set-pieces. We hoped that we would not be too despondent for our next game, the local derby match against Blackburn Rovers. We needn't have worried, as the whole team was up for it. We won 3-0 and Ashley Barnes managed to upset the TV interviewers by saying "it is always good to win, but especially against the Bastards". We just loved that man!

Consistently Excellent

After the defeat at Sheffield United, we won our next ten games – which was a record for the Championship. We had some really exciting players in the squad (Tella, Zaroury, Benson, Maatsen) together with some polished defenders (Beyer, Ekdal). Apart from sticking five past Wigan, we also scored four against Swansea, Sunderland and Huddersfield. A particular highlight was Scott

Twine's late winner against West Bromwich Albion, directly from a free kick.

As we moved into the Spring, it was clear that we were going to be promoted, it was just a question of "when". Our 2-1 away victory at Middlesbrough confirmed our promotion with seven games still to play (another Championship record) – but could we win the title?

We turned up for the home match with Queen's Park Rangers knowing that a victory would mean we were champions. We proceeded to lose that game, only the third loss throughout the season. As a result of that, we would have to try and win the title by beating our opponents in the next match – away at Blackburn Rovers! The only goal of this televised game was a signature far post curler from Manuel Benson. So, we had won the title at the home of our big local rivals!

Football League Championship : 2022-23						
		P	W	D	L	Pts
1.	Burnley	46	29	14	3	101
2.	Sheffield United	46	28	7	11	91
3.	Luton Town	46	21	17	8	80
4.	Middlesbrough	46	22	9	15	75

"Tippy Tappy" in the Six Yard Box

The 2022-23 season had been a tremendous success, with Burnley gaining 101 points, easily the best side in the division. We had played attractive football, we were worthy champions and we had some wonderful memories. Only in the 1897-98 season (when they only played 30 games) had a Burnley team lost less than the 3 defeats we registered here. But our aerial frailties had only been

exposed once (by Sheffield United) and our "tippy tappy" method of playing out from our six yard box had not been punished as often as it might. I therefore looked forward very much to another season in the Premier League, but with two major misgivings:-
1. Could we hang on to our excellent loan players and
2. Would Premier League forwards punish our "tippy tappy" defensive play?

The first worry which I carried over from the previous season was answered straight away. We were not able to hang on to our loan players, Natha Tella, Ian Maatsen and Taylor Harwood-Bellis. There was certainly a lot of pre-season transfer activity, but the loss of those three loanees proved problematic.

Miserable Start

Let me be quite clear where I stand with regard to playing "tippy tappy" on the edge of our own six yard box. I was not a good centre half but I was taught that if the ball was anywhere near our own six yard box, my job was to lump the ball as hard as I could away from that six yard box. If it meant that our opponents now had possession of the ball, at least they were sixty yards away from our goal and not six yards away.

Kompany started the season by playing his newly-signed goalkeeper, James Trafford, and not the previous season's custodian, Arijanet Muric. Young Trafford did not command his area and he was told by Kompany to play "tippy tappy" football instead of clearing his lines. Our Premiership opponents sussed very early that all they had to do was stick high crosses into our box and then play a high pressing game to steal possession as we tried to play "tippy tappy". Our weaknesses were cruelly exposed and our Premier League opponents ruthlessly punished us for losing possession.

We became the second team in English League history to lose our first seven home games and we were permanently in the bottom three. We were trying to play Manchester City's way, but without Manchester City's players.

Our first victory was away at Luton and our first home victory, on 2nd December, was 5-0 against the only team worse than ourselves, Sheffield United. Meanwhile, we had conceded three goals against Manchester City, Aston Villa, Brentford and Arsenal. We leaked four against Chelsea and five against Spurs. Once again, the only home match I missed during the season was the Boxing Day fixture against Liverpool.

To give myself a break from the driving, I had purchased train tickets for three games before Christmas and I had to cancel all three as industrial action was called. I vowed not to bother again. The actual driving has been easier since I converted to an automatic car, it is just tiring to be constantly driving in wet and dark conditions – and it is especially miserable to be doing so when your team is getting battered every week.

Miserable Middle

Our second victory was achieved in December at Fulham but before our next win at home to Brentford, we managed just three points from ten games. We simply did not learn from our mistakes, consistently losing possession in our own half and consistently getting punished for it.

For me, the worst point was reached in mid February during a 5-0 home defeat by Arsenal. Too many of our players honestly looked as if they didn't care any more, which is the biggest crime my team's players can commit. I want the players to care as much as I do and I want them to be just as heartbroken as me whenever we lose. Where was the spirit and determination that we used to get from the sides produced by Ternent and Dyche?

Miserable Ending

Our only victory in the last nine games was away at bottom club Sheffield United. Kompany dropped Trafford and brought Muric back in his place. Generally this worked well, apart from two absolute howlers against Everton and Brighton – the first was caused by Muric getting caught playing "tippy tappy" and the second was a back pass which he failed to control.
We achieved some creditable draws at West Ham, Chelsea and Manchester United – but the damage had been done.

Down Again

After the point at Old Trafford, we were thrashed 4-1 at home by Newcastle and then relegation was confirmed after a 2-1 defeat at Tottenham. In our final game, struggling Nottingham Forest came to Turf Moor and our old boy, Chris Wood, scored both goals in their 2-1 victory.

	Premier League : 2023-24					
		P	W	D	L	Pts
17.	Nottingham Forest	38	9	9	20	32
18.	Luton Town	38	6	8	24	26
19.	Burnley	38	5	9	24	24
20.	Sheffield United	38	3	7	28	16

The season had been an absolute nightmare and we went down with Luton and Sheffield United, the two sides who had been promoted with us 12 months previously.

We weren't unlucky to go down, we genuinely were the second worst side in the division. We often played some decent stuff going forward – Luca Koleosho, Wilson Odobert were lively youngsters, while Sander Berge and Jacob Bruun Larsen had been good signings. In defence, Maxime Esteve showed promise and, despite his two howlers, Muric had improved the side.

But the fundamental problem could not be ignored – we were unable to keep possession and we got punished ruthlessly. I was also annoyed that Luton and Nottingham Forest regularly showed more fight than we did.

Post-Season Developments

Vincent Kompany's reward for getting Burnley relegated was one of the top jobs in Europe, the Head Coach for Bayern Munich. I was amazed that he would be offered that role, but I do not criticise him for accepting it. When a job like that is offered, of course he has to accept it. He did not learn his lessons at Burnley and that cost us our Premier League status. But Kompany had given us one glorious season out of two and I wish him well for the future.

As I finish this book, Burnley are now back in the Championship following the most miserable season I have known – except possibly for the season when we nearly fell out of the league. We continue to ride the football roller coaster and, no matter what has gone on before, I will still look forward to supporting my beloved Burnley, even if I do live 170 miles away.

UP THE CLARETS

CHAPTER 23

WHY I DON'T HATE BASTARD ROVERS

"Diouf is a master of the dark art of the winger. He draws you in, he sucks you off." (Garry Birtles)

"If history repeats itself, I should think we can expect the same thing again." (Terry Venables)

When I was planning this book, I recognised that most Burnley fans will turn to this chapter first – even if it is near to the end of the book!

To qualify as a Claret, one of the tests appears to be a genuine hatred of Blackburn Rovers – the club, the players and the fans. And there is the suggestion that you cannot claim to be a true Claret if you cannot confirm that hatred. I therefore want to state my position, and why I feel that way.

The first FA Cup Final I watched on television with my dad was the 1960 game between Wolves and Blackburn. At that time, Wolves were big rivals of Burnley and my dad nearly always supported the underdogs, so we both sat and cheered for Blackburn – although there wasn't much to cheer, as they were well beaten, 3-0. It would be some years before I appreciated the fierce rivalry between Burnley and Blackburn.

As a remote Claret, I never lived near to any Blackburn fans, never came across Blackburn fans in school and never had to work alongside Blackburn fans. So I have not grown up with rival fans in my face, taunting and teasing me.

Only four times in my life have I been confronted by Blackburn fans:-

Back in January 1970 a friend of mine (a Manchester United fan, but a good lad despite that) drove four of us from North Wales to Burnley for an evening FA Cup replay against Chelsea. The evening was really foggy and we managed to get lost in the outskirts of Blackburn. We passed a young woman, wound down the window and said "excuse me, do you know the way to Burnley?" Without hesitation she barked "Burnley? Never bloody heard of it." We ended up missing the kick-off, too!

When I was with Hotpoint, myself and a few colleagues spent an "away day" with the staff of our third largest customer, Powerhouse. After a successful working session, we all piled into taxis for the ride to a local restaurant. As we did so, their Purchasing Director instructed the driver "full speed to Ewood Park please". There followed an evening of banter and teasing, but no blood was spilled.

A few years after that, I was presenting Institute Of Export educational packages to one of the local schools and I noticed that their coffee mugs were emblazoned with "Hartlepool United", which I presumed to be my host's team. "Oh no", he said. "Hartlepool did some stuff with our kids last year and they gave us a pile of branded mugs as well. But that's my team on the wall behind you." I turned around to see a huge Blackburn Rovers squad photograph on the wall. I feigned horror – but not enough to put him off buying my product!

My final experience came when I attended a large gathering of business advisers at a theatre in Nottingham. The Chief Executive (and my boss' boss at the time) delivered a presentation and a positive pep talk to the audience. He then declared that his forthcoming Easter weekend would be perfect if Blackburn Rovers could pick up three points. I reacted in the only way I knew – "boo" I shouted loudly at the stage. A bit risky I suppose, but thankfully he saw the funny side.

So, these few isolated incidents represent my only contacts with the "Bastards", whom I am supposed to hate. Until Jack Walker's money changed everything, I regarded Blackburn as just another old mill town with a long football tradition. I must confess that I felt the level playing field had changed after Walker's money became such an influence and I developed the same chip on my shoulder that all Clarets fans had in those days. But this did not develop into hatred, let me explain why.

- Men who beat their wives are absolute scum – and I hate them
- Paedophiles who do disgusting things to children deserve to be castrated without anaesthetic – and I hate them
- Con men who defraud little old ladies out of their savings are despicable low life – and I hate them
- Dictators who order massacres and ethnic cleansing deserve fates worse than death – and I hate them.

But I cannot bring myself to hate someone just because they support a different football team. Football is really important to me but you have to keep things in proportion. I hope the Clarets beat the Bastards every time we meet them and I hope that the Bastards never finish above us in the league again ….. but I don't hate them!

CHAPTER 24

NEVER MEET YOUR HEROES?

"Nottingham Forest are having a bad run. They've lost six matches in a row now without winning." (David Coleman)

"I knew my England career was never going to get off the mark again when manager Graham Taylor kept calling me Tony. That's my dad's name." (Mark Hateley)

They say that you should never meet your heroes, because you will be disappointed by what you find. That advice must have referred to the shallow world of showbiz, because that certainly has not been my experience when meeting former Burnley players. Over the years I have been fortunate enough to meet a number of Clarets stars in a variety of environments.

The first player I met was full back **Billy Marshall** back in 1961. To be honest, I had not heard of him beforehand, as he had mainly been a reserve team player, but it was still exciting to meet a real live Claret.

It was over 20 years before I met another Claret and it was outside Sincil Bank stadium at Lincoln. I arrived very early for Burnley's important match against our promotion rivals and my claret and blue scarf was spotted by our Assistant Manager, and former legend, **Frank Casper**. "Are you alright for a ticket, pal?" he asked. When I said that I wasn't, he handed a comp over. I did actually meet Frank again, in 1995 at a Cliviger pub with Allen Rycroft. He was excellent company. Also with us that night was our midfielder, **Adrian Randall**. He was a player who never really attained the heights which his talent promised.

In 1982 I watched a friendly game at the home of Eye United, who played a Peterborough United "all sorts" eleven for charity. One of Peterborough's players who was there but not playing was former Claret, **Billy Rodaway**. I got chatting to him because he couldn't understand why one of the spectators was wearing a claret and blue scarf!

After a home game in 1995, I was in one of the hospitality lounges and I was briefly introduced to the manager at the time, **Jimmy Mullen** – but not long enough for a chat.

I think it was at Southend in 1995 when I found myself sitting in the directors' area near to **John Pender**. He knew Allen Rycroft (as everyone seemed to) and chatted about our slim chances of avoiding relegation.

At about the same time, I was in a sponsors' bar when I was introduced to **Jim Thomson** our Seventies centre back. I believe that he was a brewery rep at the time but couldn't have a drink with us because he had a car outside. He was amusing and interesting company.

Outside the Players' entrance at the old Saltergate ground, Chesterfield, Allen Rycroft and I found ourselves chatting with **Vince Overson**. He was particularly upset over how tight the away strip shorts were!

Fast forward to the final game of the 1997-98 season, the relegation decider against Plymouth. Allen Rycroft got tickets for myself and some of the Dublin Clarets to attend an Ex-Clarets Dinner at the Keirby Hotel in Burnley. I sat next to **Harold Rudman**, a defender from the 1940s and 1950s and I had a fascinating chat with him, comparing the game he played and the modern day game. I suggested to him that current players do not seem to instantly control the ball like players had done in his day. He defended the modern players by saying "don't forget that if a ball was played in our direction, all we had to do was let it hit our chest or thigh – and the heavy ball would drop to the floor, instantly under control. Nowadays the balls are so light they are a devil to control."

Coming back up the stairs from the loo, I bumped into **Adam Blacklaw**, our hard knock goalkeeper from the Sixties. He was a soft-spoken charming man who had plenty of time for chatting to fans.

Also at the dinner, I met club legend, **Andy Lochhead**. He also was a soft-spoken man who showed great interest in what I did for a living. I managed to hold myself back from saying "never mind what I do, Andy. Not so many years ago, I actually wanted to be you!" In about 2017, I attended a sportsman's dinner, where the guest speaker was Chelsea legend, Ron "Chopper" Harris. As a friend of mine had organised the dinner, he arranged for me to sit next to "Chopper" during the meal. I decided to ask him the question that everyone probably asks him, and I was delighted with the answer. "Come on Ron, who was the hardest player you ever played against?" "Easy", said Chopper, "Andy Lochhead. He used to retaliate even <u>before</u> I kicked him".

Our full back from the Sixties, **Freddie Smith**, was another ex-player I met that evening.

In May 2000, I was lucky enough to get a ticket for the 40th Anniversary Celebration Dinner at Turf Moor to recognise the 1960 First Division Champions. The chance to meet some of my very first heroes!

The first person to whom I was introduced was the former physio, **Jimmy Holland** – which was ironic, as Jimmy wasn't at Turf Moor in 1960. But being alongside Jimmy was the best place to be. Every ex-player arrived and made a bee-line for Jimmy, as everyone knew him. Jimmy then made a point of introducing the players to me, so I pretty much met the whole lot within half an hour.

Jimmy Holland got me to meet **John Angus, Alex Elder, Tommy Cummings, Brian Miller, John Connelly, Ian Lawson, Billy White, Trevor Meredith, Brian Pilkington and Jim Furnell**. But Allen Rycroft grabbed the man I really wanted to meet and brought him over – my boyhood hero, **Ray Pointer**, the finest number nine who ever drew breath!

They always say that your first hero remains your biggest hero. Ray had a drink with me and he chatted for quite a while, which I really appreciated. We discussed the England v Portugal game from 1961, in which Ray and John Connelly scored England's two goals. I can report that my hero, Ray Pointer, was also a very nice man.

A number of post-1960 players were also present at the dinner. I got to meet **Arthur Bellamy, Brian O'Neil and Derek Scott** during the evening, as well as former Scotland and Manchester United manager, Tommy Docherty. Tommy's son had played many times for Burnley.

Whenever Allen Rycroft accompanied me to our away games at Norwich, he would leave his car at my home near Peterborough, and I would drive the second leg of the journey to Carrow Road. On one such trip, he got me to turn off the A47 and we ended up at the home of our ex-striker **Alan Taylor**. Rycroft was trying to get as many autographs as he could in a book featuring Burnley players over the years, and Taylor was one of the ones he needed.

In March 2002, I met Allen Rycroft outside Stockport County's ground. We were to collect our tickets from the Players' entrance but we didn't know from whom. We were delighted when a smiling **Graham Branch** appeared with our tickets and he chatted for a while.

I mentioned earlier in the book that I had been able to contribute to the Brian Miller Testimonial Dinner in May

2002. As well as making my presentation to Brian, I was able to meet a number of former Clarets players. Following my presentation, a number of them actually approached me for a chat.

I was delighted to meet perhaps the finest player to play for Burnley, the genius **Jimmy McIlroy**. I didn't get long with him as he was in great demand but I appreciated his time.

I met one of our greatest goalscorers, **Willie Irvine**, and discovered his keen sense of humour. A few years later, I was able to give talkative Willie a lift up to Worsthorne.

A number of our Seventies heroes were there – **Martin Dobson, Geoff Nulty, Steve Kindon, Paul Fletcher and Mike Summerbee**. Another Seventies player present was **Rob Higgins**, who became a good friend for a number of years later. I saw lots of games sat near to Rob and I appreciated the input from an ex-professional.

In line with Brian Miller's career, there were a number of Eighties stars at the event and I got to meet **George Oghani, Steve Taylor, Billy Hamilton, Neil Grewcock, Ian Britton, Phil Malley, Ashley Hoskin, David Miller and Andy Farrell.** I was particularly pleased to meet Grewcock and Britton as it was their goals in 1987 which resulted in our survival.

The next event I attended at Turf Moor was the 30th Anniversary Dinner in May 2003, celebrating our 1973 Second Division title-winning side. I had really enjoyed the 1972-73 season and it was good to meet the heroes from that side.

In addition to Dobson, Nulty, Thomson and Fletcher, who I had met previously, I got to meet **Colin Waldron, Ray Hankin, Eddie Cliff, Alan Stevenson, Dave Thomas and Eric Probert**. I reminded Ray of his sensational debut for Peterborough (which he remembered).

The 2015-16 season was memorable as Sean Dyche's team won the Championship title and we had some excellent days at home and away. But one of my biggest thrills came in about February or March of that season. As Allen Rycroft and I were walking towards my parked car, we walked past a chap and Allen said to me "would you mind giving Jim a lift back?" Although not knowing who "Jim" was, I said that it would be no problem. Allen sat in the back, as he would be getting out first and that gave me the chance to talk with our new passenger, the former Burnley legend, **Jimmy Robson**. Jim was getting on a bit by then but he still liked to pop down the hill to Turf Moor when he could. He was very grateful for the lift but the pleasure was all mine. A lovely bloke!

My sister looked after patients who had suffered from strokes and one of her elderly patients once told her that her father had been a good footballer and had played for England. She said that she had his details on an old cigarette card. The player in question was **Jack Hill**, a captain of Burnley and England during the 1920s. When my sister told her that I was a Burnley fan, the lady insisted that I should have the cigarette card.

My only claim to "fame" is that I once appeared on the front cover of "Goal" magazine! I attended a Cardiff v Middlesbrough game in October 1970, one of the players was photographed during the pre-match warm-up, and I could clearly be seen over the player's shoulder.

APPENDIX

"If God had wanted us to play football in the clouds, he'd have put grass up there." (Brian Clough)

"I'd like to play for an Italian club – like Barcelona." (Mark Draper)

The whole point of writing an Appendix is so that you can include all the bits that don't necessarily fit into the previous chapters. I am therefore going to cover a couple of rants, followed by some nominations for best players, performances and teams.

VAR

Over the years there were a number of high-level refereeing mistakes which changed the course of matches and these were picked up very quickly via TV action replays. Examples include Diego Maradona's handball against England at the 1986 World Cup, Joe Jordan's handball against Wales in a World Cup qualifier in 1977 and Frank Lampard's over-the-line attempt against Germany at the 2010 World Cup. VAR was brought in to help eliminate instances such as these and I applauded its introduction. I agree with the use of VAR. What I don't like is the way that VAR is used.

VAR was introduced in order to identify any **"clear and obvious" refereeing errors**. Now errors which are "clear and obvious" can be spotted very quickly by mere fans like myself, so expert referees can spot them even quicker. If it takes minutes to reach a decision then the error cannot be "clear and obvious", so the onfield decision should stand. I believe that the VAR official should be given no more than 20 or 30 seconds to identify errors and if the evidence to overturn the decision is insufficient at that stage, then the onfield decision should stand.

Long-winded VAR decisions have ruined the game. Fans are afraid to celebrate goals, the game is held up for ages and the atmosphere deteriorates. It should be simple – if it takes ages to analyse the evidence, then it can't be "clear and obvious". So allow VAR up to 20 or 30 seconds and after that just get on with the game.

Offside

The offside rule, and the application of it, used to be so simple. Nowadays it is a shambles.

Previously, when the ball was played forwards, if an attacker was in his opponents' half and he had less than two opponents between him and the opponents' goal-line, then he was offside and the assistant referee immediately raised the flag. Nowadays, the assistant referee waits to see "if the attacker interferes with play" before raising the flag. I have two issues with this.

Previously, if an attacker was flagged offside, a free kick would be awarded to the defending side from the position at which the attacker was flagged, which might only be a few yards inside the defending team's half. Now, the free kick is awarded from the position at which the attacker "interferes with play", which may be forty yards or so nearer to the defending team's goal-line. So the defending team is being penalised.

I agree entirely with Brian Clough's sentiments regarding whether an attacker is interfering with play. Cloughie said "if one of my attackers is in the opponents' half and he is not interfering with play, I will sack him". And he is right. If an attacker is in his opponents' half then he is either seeking to reach the ball or at worst he is attracting the attention of a defender. So he is interfering with play.

Remember when the game was simple?

I have never come close to joining the 92 Club, whereby you attend a match at the grounds of all Premier and EFL clubs. I stopped attending away matches in 2017 and at that stage I had been to 55 different league grounds – plus Southend, who were a league club then, but are not at present. I have also done the old and new Wembley and the Principality Stadium in Cardiff. Here are my nominations of excellence from those 59 grounds.

Best Goal Ever Seen
George Best for Fulham at Peterborough in 1976

Best Burnley Goal Ever Seen
Martin Paterson (play-off semi-final) at Reading in 2009

Best Performances by Burnley players
Brian Jensen at Bradford City in 2004
Glenn Little at Birmingham in 2001
Ralph Coates at home to Chelsea in 1970

Best Performance Against Burnley
Cesc Fabregas for Arsenal in 2009

Best Performance in Any Other Match
Colin Bell (Man City) at Man United in 1972
David Farrell (Peterborough) at home to Barnet in 2000

Most Memorable Matches
Aston Villa v Burnley in 1973
Burnley v Orient in 1987
Reading v Burnley in 2009
Burnley v Sheffield United at Wembley in 2009
Burnley v Manchester United in 2009
Charlton Athletic v Burnley in 2016

I have had a go at selecting teams from the players I have seen over the years. Since 1959 there have been some outstanding players but they have not made any of my teams if I haven't actually seen them live. Examples which spring to mind are Tommy Cummings, Tony Morley and Lee Dixon.

There will be a number of crowd favourites who haven't been included in the Burnley teams because I only ever saw them play third and fourth division football. They may have been great club servants but can't be compared to the international players who proved themselves at high levels. So, no Ian Britton, no Roger Eli, no "Super Johnny" Francis and no David Eyres.

The 4-4-2 teams I have drawn up are
- Best Burnley Team
- Next Best Burnley Team
- Burnley Entertainers
- Burnley Hard-Knocks
- Best Non-Burnley Team

Best Burnley Team

```
                    Nick Pope

Keiron Trippier   James Tarkowski   Colin Waldron   Alex Elder

Willie Morgan     Brian O'Neil     Jimmy McIlroy   Leighton James

              Ray Pointer      Andy Lochhead
```

Drawing up a "Best Ever" Clarets team proved more difficult than I thought – that's why I had to do a "Next Best" team as well. I have chosen Nick Pope over Tom Heaton, although they were both excellent keepers.

The back four has pace as well as muscle and, of course, Trippier also has free kicks in his locker.

Midfield was the area in which I had the most problems. I actually chose a "best ever" Clarets team without Martin Dobson or Ralph Coates! But I decided that my team needed a biting ball-winner alongside Jimmy Mac, so the Bedlington Terrier got the vote. Just imagine Morgan on one wing and James on the other.

I apologise to fans of Willie Irvine but I just have to have Ray Pointer up front and big Andy alongside him.

Despite having to leave out some favourites, I am well pleased with this line-up. Outstanding keeper, pacy full backs, strong centre backs, tricky wingers, the maestro Jimmy Mac controlling midfield and two strikers who have scored over 100 Clarets goals each.

Next Best Burnley Team

```
                    Tom Heaton
  John Angus    Michael Keane    Ben Mee     Keith Newton
  John Connelly  Martin Dobson   Gordon Harris  Ralph Coates
                  Willie Irvine  Jimmy Robson
```

This team would give my "Best Ever" team a good run for its money. We still have an international class keeper, the strength of Angus on one flank and the polish of Newton on the other.

I have decided to use old partners, Keane and Mee, in central defence. That is the Michael Keane who played for Burnley, not the one who went backwards at Everton.

Look at that midfield. The pacy goalscorer on the right wing and the tireless schemer on the other. The class of Dobson allied to the power of Harris.

Up front I have picked Jimmy Robson, who scored over 100 goals for Burnley, and Willie Irvine who grabbed 29 league goals in the season before his big injury.

If my "Best" and "Next Best" teams met, I would love to see those intriguing battles between Morgan and Newton, between James and Angus, between O'Neil and Harris. The last one wouldn't be for the feint-hearted!

I would put Harry Potts and Sean Dyche in charge of those two teams. An interesting clash.

Burnley Entertainers

```
                    Brian Jensen

 Peter Noble    Steve Davis    Jordan Beyer    Ian Maatsen

 Manuel Benson  Glenn Little   Steven Defour   Maxwel Cornet

                 Danny Ings    Robbie Blake
```

My third Burnley select eleven does not include the players who are necessarily the best in their positions, but they all brought excitement and entertainment to the side.

It just has to be "The Beast" in goal, a great crowd favourite and an excellent shot-stopper. I could have put Peter Noble anywhere, but he would still score goals, even from full back. I have Ian Maatsen on the other side, probably the best of the players we have had on loan.

I maybe don't have the best tacklers in midfield but you couldn't find a more creative bunch. All four are potential match winners, making chances for others as well as scoring spectacular goals.

Up front I have resisted the temptation to include a big man, instead I have gone for Danny Ings and Robbie Blake. Maybe I could include someone like Sam Vokes on the subs bench in case I need some aerial power later on.

Ings and Blake would provide plenty of movement, ideal for Defour's defence-splitting passes. Wouldn't beat my "Best" team, but it would be good to watch. Jimmy Adamson would manage this group.

Burnley Hard-Knocks

```
                    Adam Blacklaw
  Phil Bardsley    Colin Blant    Vince Overson   Les Latcham
  Dean Marney      Kevin Ball     Joey Barton     Ted McMinn
                   Ray Hankin     Ashley Barnes
```

Having selected a team of playmakers with silky skills, I felt obliged also to compile a team of tough guys who could look after themselves.

Scottish custodian Adam Blacklaw would be my number one. He would command his area and sort out the opposing centre forward too.

A back line of Bardsley, Blant, Overson and Latcham frightens me just to think of it. They shall not pass!

I have three ball winners in midfield, plus a left winger ("Tin Man" McMinn) who specialised in winning free kicks and getting opponents sent off.

To make sure no central defenders ever sleep soundly again, I have gone for Ray Hankin and Ashley Barnes. Both regular scorers but expert at holding the ball and bringing other colleagues into play.

I am not sure how many points that team might collect, but they would certainly top most yellow card tables! Stan Ternent would have to be the man in charge of this lot.

Best "Non Burnley" Team

```
                    Peter Shilton

Jimmy Armfield   Tony Adams    Bobby Moore    Kenny Sansom

George Best     Cesc Fabregas   Colin Bell    Eden Hazard

                  Ian Rush    Erling Haaland
```

As with the "Best" Burnley team, I found this one difficult to compile as it means eliminating some outstanding players from the list.

I only ever saw Gordon Banks on the television, so Shilton gets my vote as keeper. When he was at Forest, he was the best in the world.

Armfield was polished and pacy, never seeming to panic. Adams was the master at organising back fours and Moore would get in anyone's all-time best eleven on Earth. Sansom was a player I first saw as a Crystal Palace rising star, and I was always impressed with him over the years.

Best is another player who gets in everyone's top team. If anything, I thought Fabregas was under-rated and definitely comes in as my midfield general. Colin Bell could make and score goals, but he could also tackle. And Hazard was the opponent I feared most when watching Burnley play Chelsea.

From a huge list of strikers, I have gone for Rush and Haaland. With that midfield behind them, who knows what scoring records they would break?

Those are my all-time lists and I don't expect anyone to agree with them. One of the pleasures of being a football fan is that you can pick your own club's line-up and even a fantasy eleven from other clubs, without your selections ever being tested.
So, I can put forward these teams knowing I cannot be disproved!

Considering who to include in these teams reminds me of the great matches and players I have seen over the years. I do appreciate some of the excellent players who have opposed Burnley over the years but my fondest memories have been of loyal club servants giving their all for the Clarets cause – people like Dave Merrington, Billy Ingham, Brian Flynn, Gary Parkinson, Michael Duff and Charlie Taylor.

Even now, when I drive down the Brunshaw Road hill and Turf Moor comes into sight, I get the same tingle as I got when I arrived for my first home game. To me, Turf Moor might be distant, but it is still Mecca!

INDEX

"I'm as happy as I can be. But I have been happier." (Ugo Ehiogu)

"We must have had 99 percent of the match. It was the other three percent that cost us." (Ruud Gullit)

I have not listed Burnley, Turf Moor or Peterborough in this index, as they all appear so frequently

Aberdeen 161
Adams, Tony 196
Adamson, Jimmy 28, 31, 39, 41, 47, 58, 60
Akinbiyi, Ade 61
Aldershot 65, 66
Alexander, Graham 130, 132
Anderson, Trevor 65
Albert, Florian 33
Altrincham 15
Anderlecht 169
Anfield 28, 36, 42, 137, 164
Angus, John 183, 193
Antwerp 127
Arfield, Scott 154
Argentina 33, 127
Aris Salonika 124
Armfield, Jimmy 31, 196
Arsenal 4,8,9,10,11, 30, 37, 42, 52, 54, 62, 86, 102, 107, 130, 132, 169, 164, 173, 190
Aston Villa 44, 45, 48, 50, 53, 54, 153, 173, 190
Athens 162
Athletic Bilbao 125
Atkinson, Ron 49
Austin, Charlie 140,141
Bale, Gareth 195
Ball, Alan 31, 36
Ball, Kevin 110, 195
Bangor City 20, 21
Banks, Gordon 33, 196
Bardsley, Phil 195
Barnes, Ashley 152, 159, 163, 164, 170, 195
Barnes, Ken 16

Barnet 68, 69, 90
Barnsley 118, 139, 149, 152
Barnwell, John 65
Barton, Joey 145, 154, 166, 195
Basaksehir Istanbul 161, 162
Bayern Munich 128, 175
Bebbington, Keith 30
Beckenbauer, Franz 33
Beckham, David 146
Belgium 69, 127, 156
Bell, Colin 43, 190, 196
Bellamy, Arthur 184
Benson, John 76
Benson, Manuel 170, 171, 194
Berge, Sander 175
Best, George 12, 39, 43, 64, 190, 196
Beyer, Jordan 170, 194
Biggleswade 85
Bikey, Andre 133
Bilbao 124
Birmingham 45
Birmingham City 50, 53, 69, 74, 103, 111, 133
Birmingham League 14
Birtles, Gary 176
Bishop's Stortford 74
Blackpool 8, 31, 35, 41, 42, 44, 89
Blackburn 39, 177
Blackburn Rovers 20, 25, 59, 64, 70, 87, 110, 170, 171, 176, 177, 178, 179
Blacklaw, Adam 182, 195
Blake, Robbie 114, 130, 131, 137, 194
Blakeborough, Bob 99
Blanchflower, Danny 12
Blant, Colin 37, 195
Blundell Park 110

Bob Lord Stand 158
Boleyn Ground 115
Bolton Wanderers 74, 75, 119, 137
Bond, John 16, 75
Bond, Kevin 114
Booth, Dave 67
Border Counties Floodlit League 21
Borough United 18, 19
Bournemouth 139, 162
Boyd, George 153
Bradford City 116
Bramall Lane 56
Branch, Graham 103, 116, 184
Bremner, Billy 76
Brentford 68, 104, 114, 165, 173
Brighton & Hove Albion 47, 144, 149, 154, 156, 161, 162, 174
Brimmage, Jimmy 28
Bristol 103
Bristol City 132, 154
Bristol Rovers 60, 104
Britton, Ian 81, 185, 191
Broadhead, Gerry 15
Broadhead, Tony 15
Bromsgrove 21, 44, 45, 47, 48, 50, 52, 53, 56, 57, 63, 64
Bromsgrove Rovers 13, 15, 21
Brown, John 14
Brunshaw Road 197
Buchan, Martin 76
Burnley Cricket Club 149
Burnley Miners Social Club 148
Burton Albion 161, 162
Bury 84
Butler, Bryon 93
Cadiz 125

Caldwell, Steven 130
Cambridge United 60, 75, 92, 144
Cambridgeshire Constabulary 99
Cameroon 126
Campbell, Alan 51
Campbell, Alastair 115
Cantwell, Noel 62, 63, 67
Cardiff 117
Cardiff City 17, 46, 67, 76, 162, 186
Carrott, Jasper 69
Carrow Road 111, 184
Casper, Frank 41, 45, 46, 73, 74, 75, 89, 181
Cavanagh, Tommy 76
CEEFAX 87
Celta Vigo 125
Celtic 43
Championship 169
Charlery, Ken 68
Charles, John 21
Charles, Mel 19
Charles Buchan's Football Monthly" 34
Charlton, Bobby 30, 33, 39, 43, 44
Charlton, Jack 126
Charlton Athletic 47, 60, 149, 154, 155, 190
Chelsea 27, 38, 39, 130, 156, 157, 158, 160, 163, 173, 174, 177, 183, 190, 196
Cheshire County League 14
Chester 19, 84
Chesterfield 56, 67, 78, 108, 150, 182
Chirk 16
Chirk AAA 23
Clarke, Andy 69
Cliff, Eddie 186
Cliviger 181
Clough, Brian 22, 40, 187, 189

Coates, Ralph 31, 32, 37, 190, 192, 193
Cockfosters 86
Colchester United 103, 108
Coleman, David 180
Coleman, Sean 94
Collins, Doug 41
Collins, Nathan 169
Colwyn Bay 18, 23
Comfort, Alan 81
Companies House 117
Comstive, Paul 85
Conde, Jim 20
Connelly, John 9, 31, 183, 184, 193
Conroy, Mike 89
Conwy 18
Cooke, Andy 104, 107
Cooke, Robbie 66
Cooper, Tommy 35
Coppell, Steve 133
Cornet, Maxwell 165, 169, 194
Cotterill, Steve 117, 118, 119
Coventry City 31, 58, 74, 112, 118, 139
COVID 163
Cowley, Danny 144
Cowley, Nicky 144
Coyle, Owen 119, 130, 131, 132, 135, 137, 152
Craven Cottage 103
Crewe Alexandra 68, 77
Crouch, Peter 168
Crowland Town 23
Crystal Palace 16, 74, 75, 103, 110, 132, 149, 157, 196
Cummings, Tommy 31, 183, 191
Cwmbran 46
Czechoslovakia 57
Davies, Alan 22

Davies, Paul 87
Davis, Steve 108, 194
De Koninck 127
Deepdale 47, 84, 155
Defour, Steven 156, 160, 194
Derby 133
Derby County 41, 51, 56, 107, 116, 152, 154
Dixon, Lee 191
Dobson, Martin 37, 38, 41, 57, 73, 185, 186, 192, 193
Docherty, Mick 37, 56
Docherty, Tommy 83
Dodd, Ken 35
Doncaster 145
Doncaster Rovers 76, 140
Donovan, Terry 75
Doran, Keiron 114
Dougan, Derek 51, 62
Dover 99
Draper, Mark 187
Driffield 34
Dublin 126
"Dublin Clarets" 94, 99, 104, 114, 182
Duff, Michael 130, 197
Duffy, Gerry 19
Dundee 128
Dunn, David 110
Düsseldorf 128
Dyche, Sean 141, 150, 151, 152, 154, 155, 156, 157, 161, 164, 166, 167, 174, 186, 193
Eagles, Chris 130, 138
Edgbaston 102
Edgeley, Brian 15
Edwards, Neville 9, 11, 14, 17
Ehiogu, Ugo 199
Eintracht Frankfurt 34

Ekdal, Hjalmar 170
Elder, Alex 17, 29, 183, 192
Eli, Roger 191
Elias, Dyfed 19
Elland Road 151
Elliott, Wade 130, 135
Ellis, Terry 13
Emirates Stadium 137
England 17, 20, 33, 34, 57, 126, 128, 186, 188
Esteve, Maxime 175
Ethelston Cup 13, 13
Europa League 161
Eusebio 33
Evans, Alun 36
Everton 3, 28, 29, 34, 35, 36, 37, 41, 52, 157, 161, 162, 167, 174, 193
Evesham United 15
Ewood Park 25, 75, 155, 178
Eye United 23, 182
Eyres, David 90, 91, 191
Fabregas, Cesc 190, 196
Facebook 122
Farmer, Ted 30
Farrar Road 20
Farrell, Andy 185
Farrell, David 69, 190
Fean, Sir Vincent 103, 135, 155
Firm, Neil 66
Fleetwood 144
Fletcher, Paul 44, 185, 186
Fletcher, Steven 138
Flynn, Brian 197
France 127, 128
Francis, John 89, 90, 191
Francis, Trevor 51

Fry, Barry 68, 69, 70
Fulham 45, 59, 60, 64, 103, 110, 114, 135, 149, 164, 173, 190
Furnell, Jim 183
Gascoigne, Paul 97, 112
Gateshead 62
Gawne, Robert 20, 38, 51
Gay Meadow 17
Germany 112, 188
Gillingham 63, 106, 109
Glanford Park 109
Glasgow 39
"Goal" magazine 186
Gobowen 9, 14, 17
Godbold, Pat 113
Gomez, Nuno 101
Goodison Park 36
"Grandstand" 8
Grantham 149
Graves, Francis 39
Gray, André 154
Greaves, Jimmy 33, 191
Greig, John 40
Grewcock, Neil 81, 185
Griffin Park 114
Grimsby Town 110, 112, 113
Gudmundsson, Johann Berg 156
Gullit, Ruud 198
Gynn, Micky 66
Haaland, Erling 196
Hajduk Split 17
Halifax Town 84, 128
Halsall, Mick 68
Hamburg 26, 112, 113
Hamilton, Billy 75, 185

Hands, Greg 52
Hankin, Ray 22, 47, 66, 186, 195
Harris, Gordon 32, 193
Harris, Ron 183
Hartlepool United 178
Hartshead Moor 147
Harvey, Colin 37
Harwood-Bellis, Taylor 172
Hateley, Mark 180
Hawthorns, The 52
Hazard, Eden 157, 196
Heath, Adrian 90, 102
Heathrow 102, 103, 110, 127
Heaton, Tom 154, 166, 192, 193
Hebden Bridge 147
Helm, John 123
Hendrick, Jeff 156
Hereford United 79
Higgins, Rob 59, 134, 135, 185
Highbury 86
Highfield Road 31
Hill Freddie 63
Hill, Jack 186
Hill, Jimmy 31
Holbeach United 22
Holland, Jimmy 36, 183
Holloway, Ian 129
Holt, Clive 99, 155
Hoskin, Ashley 84, 185
Hotpoint 41, 42, 43, 48, 50, 56, 57, 59, 63, 64, 66, 79, 85, 94, 115, 177
Hotpoint Social Club 42
Howe, Don 61
Howe, Eddie 139, 140
Huddersfield Town 68, 169, 170

Hughes, Charlie 15
Hughes, Geoffrey 9, 11, 14, 17
Hughes, Ken 36
Hull City 138, 152, 153, 154, 156
Hunter, Reg 19
Imran Khan 52
Ingham, Billy 197
Ings, Danny 151, 153, 194
Inter Cities Fairs Cup 34
Ipswich Town 27, 28, 65, 111, 113, 115, 118, 144
Ireland 94, 126, 127
Irvine, Willie 17, 31, 32, 34, 185, 192, 193
Italy 126
Jackson, Alan 134, 135
Jackson, Mike 166
James, Leighton 44, 57, 80, 85, 192, 193
Jensen, Brian 116, 130, 134, 190, 194
Jones, Dave 24
Johnson, Andy 111
Jones, Harold 14
Jones, Joey 23
Jones, Mick 67
Jones, Norman 15
Jordan, Joe 188
Joyce, Warren 90
Kane, Harry 158
Keane, Michael 154, 166, 193
Keegan, Kevin 120
Keirby Hotel 104, 182
Kendall, Howard 37, 125
Kidderminster Harriers 21
Kindon, Steve 39, 185
King's Cross 134, 155
Kleivert, Patrick 127
Koleosho, Luca 175

Kompany, Vincent 168, 169, 172, 174, 175
Lampard, Frank 188
"Lancashire Evening Telegraph" 79
Lansdowne Road 126
Larissa 124
Larsen, Jacob Bruun 175
Latcham,Les 195
Latchford, Bob 51
Lausanne 34
Law, Denis 30, 39
Lawrenson, Mark 67
Laws, Brian 138, 139
Lawson, Ian 183Layer Road 103
Leeds 147, 149, 150
Leeds United 22, 31, 32, 39, 51, 52, 63, 66, 139, 149, 166, 167
Leicester City 36, 43, 51, 54, 56, 99, 151, 152, 153, 157
Lincoln 142
Lincoln City 73, 74, 77, 81, 142, 143, 144, 145, 157, 181
Lineker, Gary 55, 99
Little, Glenn 109, 111, 114, 190, 194
Littleborough 147
Liverpool 3, 16, 35, 36, 45, 46, 51, 54, 74, 131, 147, 153, 156, 160, 162, 164, 173
Llandudno 13, 18, 23, 37, 38, 44
Llandudno Junction 16, 18, 20, 38
Llangollen 19
Lochhead, Andy 28, 32, 182, 192
Lomas, Steve 88
London 102, 109, 157
London Bridge 155
London Road 62
Lord, Bob 73
Lorenzo, Peter 93
Louvre 128

Luiz, David 163
Luton Town 47, 59, 118, 144, 149, 170, 171, 173, 174, 175
Maatsen, Ian 170, 172, 194
Macclesfield Town 107
Macdonald, Malcolm 53, 57
Mackay, Dave 43
Malley, Phil 185
Malofeev, Eduard 34
Malta 126
Manchester 38, 41, 74, 102, 112, 147
Manchester City 25, 43, 53, 102, 106, 112, 138, 153, 159, 160, 163, 164, 173, 190
Manchester United 3, 20, 22, 30, 31, 32, 37, 39, 41, 42, 43, 102, 111, 128, 131, 137, 160, 174, 177, 190
Mansfield Town 70, 89
Maradona, Diego 188
Marney, Dean 153, 195
Marriott, Andy 89
Marsh, Rodney 63
Marshall, Billy 27, 181
Marshall, Tommy 41
"Match Of The Day" 32, 44, 58
Matthews, Stanley 30
McCann, Chris 130, 131
McGrath, Mick 20
McIlroy, Jimmy 31, 185, 192
McKinney, Gerry 95
McMenemy, Lawrie 78
McMinn, Ted 91, 195
McNee, Keith 79
McNeil, Dwight 169
Meadow Lane 50
Mee, Ben 154, 169, 193
Mellon, Micky 109

Meredith, Billy 16
Meredith, Trevor 183
Merrington, Dave 197
Merthyr Tydfil 21
Middlesbrough 48, 66, 74, 91, 150, 151, 154, 156, 157, 171, 186
Midland League 62
Millennium Dome 109
Millennium Stadium 117
Miller, Brian 74, 76, 112, 113, 183, 184, 185
Miller, David 185
Mills, "Rocky" 92
Millwall 73, 91
Milnrow 147
Milton Keynes 115
MK Dons 154
Molineux 29, 30, 53
Mondragon 124
Moore, Bobby 33, 43, 64, 196
Moore, Ian 73, 116
Moore, Ronnie 73
Morgan, Willie 30, 31, 32, 39, 192, 193
Morley, Tony 191
Morris, Griff 79
Morris, Peter 65
Morrison, Clinton 120
Morton, George 20
Motson, John 142
Mullen, Jimmy 89, 90, 181
Muric, Arijanet 172, 174, 175
Nantwich Town 15
Napoli 20, 34
National League 144
Neenan, Joe 81
Neilson, David 99

Netherlands 127
Newark 131, 145
Newcastle United 53, 75, 166, 167, 174
Newport County 18
Newton, Keith 193
Ninian Park 46
Noble, Mark 136
Noble, Peter 43, 194
Norman Cross 98
North Korea 33
North Wales 3, 15, 16, 18, 23, 31, 32, 36, 39, 45, 46, 50, 56, 76, 79, 102, 106, 111, 155, 177
Northampton Town 76, 89, 150
Northern Ireland 17, 117
Northern Premier League 20
Norway 127
Norwich City 43, 111, 112, 114, 116, 166, 167, 170, 184
Nottingham 51, 178
Nottingham Forest 9, 22, 111, 132, 174, 180, 196
Notts County 50, 65, 92
Nulty, Geoff 41, 185, 186
Nuneaton 144
Odobert, Wilson 175
Offside 189
OFI 124
Oghani, George 84, 185
Old Trafford 36, 42, 43, 102, 137, 160, 174
Oldham Athletic 50
Olympiakos 162
O'Neil, Brian 31, 32, 184, 192, 193
ORACLE 87
Orient 44, 77, 78, 79, 81, 82, 87, 91, 135, 190
Osman, Russell 114
Oswestry 13
Oswestry Town 14, 15, 21

Overson, Vince 182, 195
Owen, Michael 142
PAOK Salonika 124
Parc des Princes 128
Paris 128
Parkinson, Gary 91, 197
Paterson, Martin 130,134, 190
Pearce, Stuart 146, 191
Pelé 34, 97
Pender, John 182
Philliskirk, Tony 90
Pickering, Ally 103
Pilkington, Brian 183
Pinto, Joao 24
Plymouth Argyle 31, 90, 104, 182
Pointer, Ray 28, 31, 184, 192
Pontefract 147
Pope, Nick 157, 166, 169, 192
Portmadoc 19
Portsmouth 138
Portugal 33
Potteries 102
Potts, Harry 193
Powell, Ivor 7
Powerhouse 178
Pozzo 150
Prestatyn 19
Preston North End 47, 84, 106, 109, 133, 139
Pride Park 107
Principality Stadium 190
Pritchard, Keith 19
Pritchard, Mike 19
Probert, Eric 37, 186
Quadrant 42
"Queen Hotel" 99

Queen's Park Rangers 44, 47, 48, 114, 152, 153, 154, 171
Racecourse 16, 17, 107
Ramsey, Alf 113
Randall, Adrian 181
Ranieri, Claudio 55
Reading 100, 103, 132, 133, 134, 190
Real Madrid 125
Redknapp, Harry 105, 114
Reeves, Kevin 75
Reims 26
Richards, John 53
Riverside Stadium 157
Roberts, Graham 72
Roberts, John 51
Roberts, Vic 14
Robertson, Jimmy 37
Robson, Bobby 49, 113
Robson, Jimmy 9, 186, 193
Rochdale 76, 84
Rodaway, Billy 181
Rodriguez, Jay 131,140
Romania 127
Rome 166
Ross, Ian 65
Rotherham United 73, 75, 89, 116, 144
Rothwell, Bernard 99
Rowley, Arthur 18
Rudman, Harold 182
Rush, Ian 101, 123, 196
Russell, Kevin 90
Ryan, Mel 15
Rycroft, Allen 97, 98, 99, 100, 104, 115, 130, 133, 135, 148, 181, 182, 183, 184, 186
Rycroft, Jeanette 99
Sainsbury's 103

Saltergate 182
Sansom, Kenny 196
Santiago Bernabeu Stadium 125
Savage, Robbie 117
Scarborough 20
Scott, Derek 184
Scunthorpe United 76, 107, 139
Seeler, Uwe 112, 113
Shearer, Alan 156
Shankly, Bill 7, 54
Shannon, Les 124
Shaw, David 50
Sheffield 147
Sheffield United 133, 134, 135, 164, 170, 171, 172, 173, 174, 175, 190
Sheffield Wednesday 22, 44, 46, 75, 113, 119, 130
Sherpa Van Trophy 84, 86
Shilton, Peter 196
Shrewsbury Town 17, 18
Shropshire 9, 13, 16, 17, 18, 29
Shutt, Carl 22
Sincil Bank 181
Slack, Trevor 66
Sliema Wanderers 19
Slovan Bratislava 19
Smith, Delia 111
Smith, Freddie 183
Southall, Neville 78
Southampton 52, 149
Southend United 74, 76, 98, 182, 190
Southern League 21
Southport 144
Sowerby Bridge 147
Spain 124
Spalding United 22

Stadium Of Light 115
Stamford 149
Stamford Bridge 156, 158, 163
Stamford Town 21, 22
Stansted 103
Steele, Eric 65
Stelling, Jeff 158
Steven, Trevor 74
Stevenage 85
Stevenson, Alan 186
St.Andrews 111
St.John, Ian 28
St.Johnstone 119, 128
St.Martins 9, 13, 14
Stockport County 68, 91, 103, 112, 184
Stoke City 29, 35, 103, 135, 157, 159, 160
Stokes, Amber 69, 79
Stokes, Ceri 67, 68
Stokes, Clive 46
Stokes, Derek 13
Stokes, Eric 14, 27, 29
Stokes, Fred 46
Stokes, Jim 8
Stokes, Travis 13
Storefjell 127
Strachan, Gordon 129
Strawbs, The 53
Stuttgart 34
Summerbee, Mike 185
Sunderland 46, 115, 117, 118, 170
Swansea City 156, 170
Swindon Town 37, 43
Tarkowski, James 166, 169, 192
Taylor, Alan 184
Taylor, Charlie 197

Taylor, Graham 180
Taylor, Steve 185
Teasdale, Frank 99
Tella, Nathan 170, 172
Ternent, Stan 17, 104, 105, 106, 108, 109, 110, 111, 114, 117, 118, 147, 174, 195
Thomas, David 39, 186
Thomas, Gwynedd 51
Thomas, Mickey 23
Thomas, Mitchell 136
Thompson, Steven 134
Thomson, Jim 41, 182, 186
TNS 15
Todd, Sammy 17
Todmorden 147
Torquay United 16, 66, 77, 87
Toshack, John 17
Tottenham Hotspur 11, 25, 27, 28, 29, 43, 74, 86, 90, 131, 158, 159, 160, 163, 165, 166, 173, 174
Trafford, James 172
Tranmere Rovers 84
Treacy, Keith 70, 140
"Trinity Inn" 94
Trippier, Keiron 192
Truswell, Nigel 135
Turner, Chris 63, 65, 67, 68
Twine, Scott 170, 171
Twitter 122, 140, 169
Tyler, Martin 88
Ure, Ian 30
U.S.A. 126
Valencia 125
Valley, The 155
VAR 188
Venables, Terry 83, 176

Venison, Barry 168
Verso, Graham 95
Victoria Road 14, 15
Viduka, Mark 105
Villa Park 45, 53, 54
Vindheim, Rune 103
Vokes, Sam 151, 154, 156, 158, 194
Waddle, Alan 66
Waddle, Chris 102, 104
Wagstaff, Dave 53
Wakefield 90
Walcott, Theo 72
Waldron, Colin 41, 47, 186, 192
Wales 17, 20, 22, 33, 38, 117, 156, 188
Walker, Jack 178
Walsall 103, 112
Watford 103, 110, 113, 114, 116, 150, 151, 163, 167, 170
Weghorst, Wout 166
Welsh Premier League 15
Wem Town 14
Wembley 57, 68, 69, 84, 85, 86, 90, 91, 100, 131, 134, 158, 159, 190
West Bridgford 51
West Bromwich Albion 26, 50, 52, 53, 66, 132, 153, 158, 171
West Germany 57
West Ham United 11, 16, 43, 63, 115, 138, 161, 166, 174
Whitchurch & District League 13, 14
White, Billy 183
Whixall 14
Wigan Athletic 20, 152, 170
Wile, John 22, 66
Williams, Les 38, 39, 44, 45, 46, 47, 155
Williams, Ted 29
Willian 157

Wilson, Ray 33
Wimbledon 115, 145
Wolverhampton Wanderers 9, 25, 26, 29, 30, 31, 38, 50, 51, 52, 53, 57, 84, 85, 86, 133, 164, 177
Wood, Chris 158, 164, 166, 174
Workington 18
World Cup 1966 32
Worsthorne 185
Wrexham 16, 17, 18, 19, 23, 27, 65, 107, 109
Wright, Ian 108, 109
Wrigley, Wilf 37
Wycombe Wanderers 102, 106
Yaxley 23
York City 87
Zaroury, Anass 170
Zola, Gianfranco 150
Zurich 17

By The Same Author

Business networking has become an increasingly important element within the marketing strategy of a business but, like all marketing activities, it needs to be planned, structured and measured if it is to be effective.
Having been a prolific networker and the creator of innovative networking events over a number of years, Mike Stokes has seen some of the best networkers in action – and some of the worst!
This book helps new and inexperienced business networkers to
- find the most appropriate networking groups for their businesses
- understand how to network effectively
- recognise the mistakes that poor networkers make

It also assists organisers of networking events by
- outlining how to establish and grow a networking group
- suggesting how rounds of elevator pitches can be spiced up
- explaining how to set up and run 20 different networking formats

The book introduces networkers to The 5 Ps of Networking and it gives leaders of networking groups a stack of new ideas.
If your networking is NOT working, it is almost certainly your own fault, and this book explains why.

By The Same Author

Mike Stokes has seen or committed every mistake in the exporting book, initially as a successful exporter and more recently as an export adviser. He is perfectly placed therefore to guide new and potential exporters around the various pitfalls which exist.

This is not just a "How To Export" book, it is full of anecdotes and observations which have been gathered over a long and rewarding career in international trade. It is the kind of book that can only have been written by someone who has the bruises to show for his troubles.

Tips are given on market selection, export pricing, preparing for foreign trips, negotiating across different cultures and how to use overseas exhibitions. These are the reflections of someone who spent 38 years armed with just a passport, an order pad and a key to the minibar!

www.ingramcontent.com/pod-product-compliance
Lightning Source LLC
Chambersburg PA
CBHW072154070526
44585CB00015B/1136